COURAGE to FOLLOW the VISION

The Journey of Lyle Emerson George

COURAGE TO FOLLOW THE VISION

by TOM WILSON

 RED APPLE
PUBLISHING

FIRST EDITION

RED APPLE
PUBLISHING
15010 113ᵀᴴ St. KPN
Gig Harbor, WA 98329-5014
(253) 884-1450

Printed by Gorham Printing
Rochester, WA 98579

ISBN 1-880222-47-7
Library of Congress Control Number: 2001098170

Cover art by Danny Shaw
Text and cover design by Kathryn E. Campbell

Disclaimer: Although the author, storyteller, and publisher have tried to
ensure accuracy and completeness of the events, they assume no
responsibility for errors, inaccuracies, omissions or any inconsistencies.
Events are colored by the author's and storyteller's viewpoint and how
they affected them.

About the cover art: The totem on the cover is a drawing of the exact
totem carved for the 1962 Seattle World's Fair by Joe Hilliar, a
Suquamish Indian who was a neighbor of Mr. George's. Later, the totem
"toured" the United States and was even exhibited in Seattle's sister city,
Kobe, Japan.

The gravesite pictured on the cover is an exact rendition of Chief
Seattle's gravesite on the Suquamish Reservation.

DEDICATION

To Lyle Emerson George, a remarkable human being,
driven by a desire to educate and enlighten. As a leader of his
people, he displays great foresight and wisdom. He knows that
understanding comes from truth, and truth depends on the
absence of fear and ignorance.

To that end, I dedicate this book . . . and with all due respect
and admiration, I call him Emerson.

INTRODUCTION

Lyle Emerson George and I met at work. We each had our own cubicle at opposite ends of a hallway. I passed by him daily, paying him little mind. One of my collateral tasks is publishing a small shop newsletter. The material is mostly work related and a bit dry to say the least. I try to include articles of non-work-related material or humor just to break things up. I had purchased a book by Chief Dan George, the actor. The book was called *My Heart Soars* and was full of poems and short stories from the author's perspective. I have always been a big fan of Chief Dan George. He played Old Lodge Skins in the movie *Little Big Man* opposite Dustin Hoffman. He was also a main character in *The Outlaw Josey Wales* starring Clint Eastwood. I considered putting a poem from his book in the newsletter, but I was a bit concerned about possible copyright infringement. The thought crossed my mind that maybe Lyle Emerson George was somehow related to Chief Dan George. Never one to hold my tongue, forked as it may be, I walked back to his cubicle, plopped myself down in his guest chair, and introduced myself. He looked up, smiled, and extended his hand, "I'm Lyle George."

I got directly to the point. "I was wondering if you were related to Chief Dan George the actor?"

He smiled. "Chief Dan George," he said.

I would learn later that Lyle often answered by repeating part of my question. He says it's an excellent way to ensure that what you think you heard is what the other person actually said, or something like that. Either way, I came to depend on the affirmation.

Lyle told me a story, another trait I found intriguing. His eyes studied my face as he spun his tale. He spoke like a man of many stories. His words and inflections were precise and deliberate, and there was a colorful hint of ethnic phrasing. His sincerity was genuine and left little for me to question.

"My great-great-grandmother," he said, "was taken from her home in Canada by a Makah raiding party. She was only four years old. The Makah brought her back to their village as a slave. The Makah were not mean to their slaves. Slaves were valued property. She was tasked with keeping the fire and cleaning up after the animals. Eventually, she was traded to the S'Klallam Tribe at Little Boston. She met and married my great-great-grandfather, who was cousin to Chief Dan George. I have a picture of him somewhere. He looks exactly like Chief Dan George . . . the spittin' image."

I asked him if he thought that it would be okay to put the poem in the newsletter. "If you are reprinting the poem and crediting him as the author," he offered, "I don't think there would be any problem."

"It never hurts to ask a blood relative," I said, and we both laughed.

I asked him if he wanted to read a couple of short stories I had written that I thought he might find interesting.

He said yes.

As a writer, I liked this guy more and more by the minute. I handed him a disk and asked him to read the file called *Selected Shorts*. He sat in his chair and read while I watched his face to catch his every expression.

"Say, Chief, this is a nice place ya got here, the valleys and streams; the mountains and forests; the wildlife and precious minerals . . . amazing. Yes, sir, a mighty nice place. Ya know, Chief, it come to me the other day that there don't appear to be enough room here fer the both of us, so the way I got it figured one of us has gotta go. Tell ya what, why don't you gather up yer people, take this case of alcohol and this here bundle of smallpox-infected blankets and go find yerself another place ta hang out."

Lyle smiled the entire time he was reading. "Very good," he said, "I like the way you think. My grandpa was Benny George. He died on Veterans Day, 1971. When I was a small boy, knee high to a grasshopper, Grandpa had me go up into the woods and selectively limb a cedar tree, lash the limbs in a bundle, and take them down to the beach. The next morning at low tide we all took our buckets down to dig clams. When we finished digging, he had me drag the bundle of limbs down to the water's edge, lash them together, put them upright in the hole, and then fill the hole with sand. When I asked my grandpa why we were planting the limbs he said, "When the tide comes in, the limbs will be a good place for the herring to lay their eggs. Always remember, boy, never take anything without putting something back."

I paused . . . long enough for the story to sink in. "That's excellent!" I said. "Never take anything without putting something back."

"Without putting something back," he echoed.

Lyle and I walked out together that night. I expressed an interest in capturing some of his stories for posterity. He agreed, and we arranged to meet at a local restaurant later that week. Over dinner, Lyle talked and I listened.

"First, let me start by telling you who I am. I am Lyle Emerson George. While growing up, I was Emerson. In the Service, I was George. In my professional life, I am Lyle. To my friends and family, I am Emerson. I've come to the conclusion that there is a specific reason why I do that; I keep my work 'work' and I keep my personal life 'personal'—to the point of using different names. The meeting I attended just before I came here to meet you was with a counselor that I see every two weeks. I grew up in an alcoholic environment. There are abnormalities from those times that seem to follow me, so I deal with those issues on a regular basis. The meeting that I was going to go to after we finish tonight is called Adult Children of Alcoholics. It's a group of folks who share the same experiences. I can go there, feel comfortable, and talk about what I need to talk about. Alcohol is really prevalent in the family. I choose to do something about it.

"The traditional greeting of my people is to recite your lineage. My grandpa was Edwin George, Senior. My grandma was Martha Louise George. My mother was Doralee Deam from Arkansas, and my father was Lyle Merel Edwin George, born on our driveway on the family homestead. I was born in 1950 in the old Harrison Memorial Hospital, and I have a younger brother, Greg."

"Your mother was from Arkansas? What tribe?"

He smiled. "The Caucasian Tribe."

"I've been married for twenty-six years to a wonderful woman, Sue, and we have three children. The oldest one is into computers. He was in the Army during Desert Storm. Number two is a trooper for the Washington State Patrol, and number three is studying Speech and Hearing Science at the University of Washington. One of our granddaughters, Brianna, is two this year, and our newest granddaughter, Madeline, was born on the 4th of September 2000.

"The George clan is very large. You can't travel far in Suquamish without running into the name George. If you head out of Poulsbo on Highway 305 towards the Agate Pass Bridge and Bainbridge Island, you'll see several different sizes of fire-work stands all emblazoned with the name George. I own one of the smaller stands. If you look really close, you will find Georges selling cut wood and smoked salmon. So, it's generally accepted that the George clan is Suquamish. However, that is not really true. Grandma Martha was the only true Suquamish. Indians follow their father's lineage. All of my aunts and uncles as well as my Grandpa Benny were Port Gamble S'Klallam. When Benny of the Port Gamble S'Klallam and Martha of the Suquamish were married, the family had blood in both tribes. Under tribal law, family members can "switch" affiliation. When I was old enough to decide such things, I switched from the Port Gamble S'Klallam to the Suquamish Tribe. My father and about three-quarters of the George clan followed suit.

"In the Indian culture, the perception of ownership differs greatly from the White perception of ownership. To the Indians, buying and selling land is abstract, like buying and selling the air. The land is their mother, providing them with sub-sistence . . . it is something to be cared for and respected. To the Whites, the own-ership of land means the possession of physical wealth . . . resources that can be harvested and sold. Unfortunately the line between Indian culture and White cul-ture has become muddied over the years. The White man's fervent effort to assimi-late the Indians into White culture was carried out in God's name with great enthusiasm. There are many tribal folks who have lost the connection with their cultural identity. There are Indians on our reservation that I would not dare turn my back on, and a large percentage of them are my blood relatives. In light of that, I consider it extremely important that non-Indians understand that there are intelli-gent, educated Indian men and women who have a great deal to offer humanity.

"I was doing some research in the archives at Sand Point when I came across some very interesting documents. I have photostats of letters that my Grandma Martha wrote to the Government Man at the Bureau of Indian Affairs. She actu-ally called him the Government Man. She wrote in one letter that she needed $13.00 to get through the month to buy flour, coffee, beans and other staples. What I found ironic is that my grandma, who was Suquamish, and my aunt and two of my uncles, who were still Port Gamble S'Klallam at the time, came up with the idea of selling cigarettes on the reservation . . . not a bad idea. They bootlegged cigarettes and sold them tax-free. They turned a healthy profit until the IRS showed up and presented them with a sizeable tax bill from Uncle Sam. They owed the Government

Man a lot of money. My grandma was the licensee. She was the responsible party. Two of the other three didn't pay a cent in taxes. They had loans against their businesses and their homes and everything else of value, but they skated out of paying because the property they used as collateral couldn't be touched . . . it was on the Indian reservation . . . it was Trust Property . . . the Government Man already owned it. The representative from the District Office of the Bureau of Indian Affairs in Everett said, 'Martha George owns sixty-two feet of no-bank waterfront; go put a lien on it.' They put a lien on my grandma's property for the money she owed in taxes from the sale of cigarettes. The lien was in direct violation of the trust agreement between Indian tribes and the agencies of the United States Government that are supposed to represent us . . . a direct contradiction.

"Let me tell you about the historical massacre at Pine Ridge in the 1800s. A Piyute spiritual leader, a medicine man, was preaching the traditional native gospel, and a spiritual dance called the Ghost Dance was performed as a part of that religious ceremony. The medicine man was traveling about the territory spreading the word. (A guy named Jesus did that too.) He was at Pine Ridge where he came upon a man they called Bigfoot who was born with a clubfoot . . . just a stump, no toes. The medicine man was praying to give good medicine to Bigfoot. He started performing the Ghost Dance, a marathon dance. I don't remember if they used peyote or not, but it is an enhancing dance meant to raise the spirits. The Cavalry witnessed the ceremony and assumed that, since this was now a reservation, the Indians must be getting ready to go to war. The soldiers came on the reservation and told the Indians to knock it off. The medicine man continued the ceremony, and it led to the massacre of hundreds of Indians, mostly old men, women and children.

"At Wounded Knee in 1975, the Federal Government had an issue with what they thought was a group of modern-day rabble-rousers. The natives on the reservation took up arms. There was a confrontation and two FBI Agents were killed. Leonard Peltier, one of the leaders of the American Indian Movement (AIM), and two other Indians were singled out as principal suspects. The FBI immediately arrested the two others. They were both tried. The evidence for the defense was overwhelming. An all-White jury acquitted both men. Leonard Peltier was eventually captured in Canada and extradited to the United States for his trial. For some reason, the trial judge ruled that all evidence, except the events that occurred the day of the actual incident, would be excluded from his trial. In a blatant miscarriage of justice, critical information that lead to the acquittal of the other two suspects was not allowed at the trial of Leonard Peltier.

"The Leonard Peltier Defense Committee claimed that the FBI had singled out Peltier as a leader of AIM and had made him and other AIM leaders the focus of government efforts directed at silencing AIM through attacks and arrests. A key Indian eyewitness for the prosecution during the trial later freely admitted that his statements were coerced . . . that the FBI threatened, terrorized, and harassed him and his family. The jury convicted Leonard Peltier of the murders. He is still in prison serving two consecutive life sentences . . . locked up for a quarter of a century. Numerous investigations have been conducted, and there is conclusive evidence that Leonard Peltier was not responsible for the deaths. Robert Redford produced the documentary *Incident at Oglalla* in support of Peltier's innocence.

"There is, and has been for some time, a popular movement to free Leonard Peltier . . . get him out of prison. Amnesty International urged President Clinton to pardon Peltier. President Clinton promised to look at the Peltier case before he left office as part of an overall review of clemency cases. Citizen Bill Clinton and his wife, Senator Hillary Rodham Clinton (D-N.Y.), walked away from the White House on the 20th day of January 2001. On his last day as President, Clinton issued pardons to one hundred and forty Americans, including his brother and the individuals who were indicted and convicted in the Whitewater real estate scandal that marred his presidency. Leonard Peltier's name was not on the list. That struggle is still ongoing . . . get Leonard Peltier out of prison. FBI agents were killed, but many people say that the killings were justified. You know, self defense . . . the Rodney King angle."

Lyle told of how he had resigned as the Suquamish Tribal Council Chairman because the Tribal Council lacked the courage to follow the vision and how, at one point, he had feared for his life and the lives of his wife and children. He smiled as he shared the story of when he and his friends had found the previously undiscovered trail blazes left by the 1889 Press Expedition into the Olympic Mountains. He spoke proudly of his participation as a member of the National Indian Council and of the day he presented a Red Eagle feather to Senator John McCain of Arizona to recognize him as a wounded warrior and friend of the Indians. He discussed everything from Chinook Jargon, tribal gaming, boundary disputes, salmon, and legal battles over tidelands to assimilation, anarchy, lawlessness, drugs, alcoholism, poverty, and corruption on the reservation.

When our interviews were over, I sat in my chair and reviewed tape after tape of material. I spent countless hours writing this book. I retold Lyle's story in the third person. When I was finished, the book didn't work. It was very depressing. I knew the material was good, but for some reason it just didn't flow. Then it came to me. The best way to share these stories was to act as a medium. My ego was in the way. I had concentrated so hard on trying to be an excellent storyteller that I forgot about the guy who was telling the stories. I changed the entire text to first person and it all flowed together. I hope you find the following pages as engaging and enlightening as I have.

—JTW

CONTENTS

1 | The Great White Canoe

TODAY, IN THE LATE SUMMER AND EARLY FALL, THE KICKER BOATS ARE thick off Point Jefferson, also known as Jeff Head. The locals are fishing for the salmon that migrate in from the ocean and make their way along the shore to their spawning grounds in the streams and rivers of the South Sound. The view from Jeff Head is spectacular. You can see up and down the coastline to the north and south, and across the water the emerald city of Seattle sparkles like a jewel in the setting sun.

Long before the Whites came to the Northwest, the Suquamish camped along the shores of Puget Sound in an inland bay just to the west of Jeff Head. The Suquamish were a peaceful people but you wouldn't want to mess with them. If they were threatened, they would fiercely defend their homes and families.

The point at Jeff Head was an ideal location for spotting the canoes of Indian raiding parties. The tribe positioned young boys at Jeff Head. Their job was to act as sentries and give advance warning of an impending attack. They were called crane boys. Being chosen for the job was a great honor. If the crane boys spotted the canoes of a war party, they would run full speed toward the village making the sound of a crane. Their warning would signal the women to gather up their kids and hide in the woods while the tribal warriors prepared for battle.

In 1792 the tribe was alerted by the call of the crane boys. Chief Sealth was seven at the time. His dad was Schweabe, Chief of the Suquamish. There was a terrible commotion coming from down on the beach. Sealth rushed down to the water and ran to his father's side. He looked out across the bay and gazed in disbelief. An apparition appeared from the mist. It had wings that fluttered like a giant bird. The men grabbed their weapons. The women and children ran into the woods. Sealth stood his ground at his father's side.

Kitsap was War Chief of the Suquamish. He was first to notice that there were men climbing on the back of what appeared to be a big canoe. The large ship slowed and dropped anchor. Chief Schweabe and Kitsap pushed a canoe into the surf. They quickly approached the strange vessel. The two men paddled a complete circle around the large canoe to protect themselves from evil spirits. Schweabe knew that these strange men must be very brave to climb so high on the ropes and wooden beams. He yelled out a greeting. The men on the giant canoe responded. Schweabe did not understand their words, but he could sense by their gestures and demeanor that they intended his people no harm.

The next morning the Indians loaded their canoes with a bounty of food and gifts. The men paddled out to the great boat. Sealth would not be left behind with the women and children and sat in the canoe at his father's side. Each canoe circled the boat and then pulled alongside. The Indians were very impressed with the men who stood tall on the wooden decks. They had white faces, and their hair was many colors. Sealth was particularly delighted with one well-dressed, pale-faced man with blue-gray eyes and a warm, friendly smile. The man placed his hand on the young boy's head and spoke to him in a warm gentle tone. Young Sealth had just met 33-year-old Captain George Vancouver of the sailing ship *Discovery*. He was completely captivated. A great potlatch was held. The Suquamish people presented these strange white men with many gifts. In return, they were given wondrous presents of beads and buttons. From that point forward, life for the Northwest Indians was never the same.

2 | The Old Man House

MY ANCESTORS WERE A NOMADIC PEOPLE. THEY MOVED FROM PLACE to place with the cycle of the sun and moon. Everything had a rhythm . . . a seasonal rhythm . . . time for berries and a time for salmon . . . a time for shellfish and a time for venison. In the cold and rainy months, the tribe would cram into their crude winter quarters on Blake Island. Chief Schweabe sat by the fire one evening as a heavy rain fell outside. The roof of the shelter was far from waterproof, and he watched as his men, cold and wet, pushed and shoved for a warm place by the fire. Forty or more dogs were jammed into the close quarters and the smell was not pleasant. Chief Schweabe was not pleased. "We will build a communal house," he proclaimed, "and it will be a grand house where our people will be warm and dry."

Chief Schweabe sent his warriors to the north and south in search of the perfect location. He himself selected the shores of the narrow Agate Passage where the saltwater flowed with the tide like a mighty river. "This is the place," he said, "where we will build Ol-e-Man."

The front of the grand house was fifteen feet high. The roof beams were made from cedar logs sixty-five feet long and more than two feet thick at the widest end. The Old Man House covered one and one-quarter acres. It was more than three city blocks long and was separated into forty apartments, each containing a massive fireplace. The building, constructed entirely by hand, was an engineering marvel. Every family had its own apartment. The apartments were divided into rooms by grass mats suspended from the ceiling. From the strategic location of the

Old Man House, a traveler could journey up the bay at flood tide and return with ease when the tide came ripping back through Agate Passage toward the ocean.

During construction Chief Schweabe and his men encountered an unexpected problem. They were unable to lift the large end of the center log the fifteen feet necessary to set it in place. The great War Chief, Kitsap, suggested that the other Puget Sound tribes be invited to Suquamish for a great potlatch. A splendid contest would be held to see which tribe could muster up the strength to lift the center log into position. Chief Schweabe sent his messengers to tell the other tribes of the great potlatch and the challenge of strength. The Snoqualmie, Muckleshoot, Puyallup, Squally, Duwamish, Snohomish, and Skykomish all showed up. Kitsap himself carried the invitation to the Squally. They all converged on Suquamish for days of feasting and ceremony.

Late that first night the mood was festive as the men of many tribes gathered around a huge bonfire. Chief Schweabe introduced his son Sealth, now a young man, to the tribal leaders. Sealth stood before this great assemblage and gave his first public speech. There was no sound other than a dog barking and the crackling of the fire. Sealth was a tall and commanding figure like his father, and he towered above the other men of his tribe. The guests leaned forward in amazement at the first sound of his rich and powerful voice.

"Welcome, friends and neighbors," he said. "Today our hearts are light. One grandfather ago such a meeting was not possible."

His voice rushed through them like the wind through the trees.

"A new day comes," he continued. "Above the water the sun, kind and warm, smiles down. Between glorious Squa-cooke (the Cascade Mountains) toward sunrise and glorious Towiat (the Olympic Mountains) toward sunset, all Red men should live like brothers."

Several prominent Tribal elders yelled out, "Hear him! Hear his words!" Young Sealth had made a lasting impression on the leaders of the Puget Sound tribes, and the foundation of a great union was born that day.

The next morning dawned, and the men from each tribe gathered in front of the Old Man House. It was time to begin the contest. There had been much boasting and many wagers as to which tribe was strong enough to lift the huge log into place. Success would surely bring great honor. Each tribe in turn sent their most powerful warriors to lift the large end of the log. All failed until there were but two tribes remaining, the Duwamish and the Suquamish.

The Duwamish made a gallant effort. Everyone was fascinated with their use of long poles for leverage. With this mechanical advantage they were able to lift the end of the log higher than any other tribe up to that point; yet, they were still inches short. The Suquamish themselves were the final contestants, and everyone knew that it was their inability to accomplish the task in the first place that had been the motivating factor for the contest. The lesson of the Duwamish was not lost on Schweabe. The men of the Suquamish, using long poles for leverage, gathered under the log, and with one enormous, final thrust, slipped the great beam over the edge of the center poles and dropped it into place. Today, on the beach in Suquamish, you can still see the remnants of the great Ol-e-Man . . . The Old Man House.

3 | Victory on the White River

THE TIME CAME FOR THE SON OF CHIEF SCHWEABE TO TAKE A WIFE. It was decided that a marital union with the beautiful maiden La Dailiá of the Duwamish would forever bond the two tribes in friendship. Chief Schweabe and Sealth traveled to the Duwamish with many gifts to offer the family of the bride, including heaping baskets of dried salmon, smoked mussels, barnacles, clams, and oysters as well as blankets of doe, beaver and ground hog. A beautiful, intricately designed blanket of thick mountain wool that had been taken from the north as a war trophy was also presented to the bride's family.

The happy couple was joined together and they traveled back to Ol-e-Man house where they would make their home. Before the honeymoon was over, the brother of La Dailiá showed up with a dire warning . . . the Duwamish had learned that fierce mountain Indians from the White River were planning a raid on the Suquamish. The mountain Indians from both the upper Green and White Rivers were very aggressive and had terrorized the saltwater tribes for generations.

Sealth and his father selected their most fearless braves. War Chief Kitsap armed the warriors with axes, clubs, bows and arrows. They met up with warriors from six other Puget Sound tribes where the White River emptied into the saltwater. That night, under the stars, the War Chiefs offered up their individual plans for battle. Each plan was discussed and rejected. Finally, twenty-two-year-old Sealth stepped forward. "We will outwit this enemy!" he proclaimed. He then masterfully outlined his strategy.

His plan was unanimously accepted, and at daybreak the assembled warriors followed Sealth to a sharp bend in the White River where a tall tree towered from the water's edge. They chopped at the tree with wedges of elk horn and yew wood, driving foot-long wedges into the heart of the trunk, and by late afternoon the tree toppled into the river, where it floated only a few inches above the surface.

Heavily armed, Sealth and the other warriors hid in the bushes. At dusk, five canoes carrying a hundred tall mountain Indians, painted for war, glided down the White River. They were moving very fast as they rounded the corner. By the time they saw the trap, it was too late to stop. Their canoes were smashed on the submerged tree, and they were thrown into the water. Sealth and the other warriors rushed out onto the log, and most of the mountain Indians were clubbed to death. Sealth would never again engage in battle, but the Grand Council was so impressed by the one-sided victory that they declared young Sealth Chief of the Allied Tribes.

Sealth and his beloved wife La Dailiá had one daughter whom they named Wee-wy-eke. She was later given the Christian name of Angeline. Sadly, La Dailiá died shortly after giving birth, but Angeline grew up, married, and had children. Today there are a handful of documented descendants from that marriage. After her death Chief Sealth took another wife, and there were many concubines. Several more children were born of those unions. One of the children was given the Christian name of George. It is difficult to trace these descendants, perhaps because the Roman Catholic Church was put in charge of the Port Madison Indian Reservation after Chief Sealth signed the Point Elliot Treaty, and the Roman Catholic Church did not recognize second marriages. And they certainly weren't in favor of concubines.

Chief Sealth was a remarkable man. He was a leader of his people and a great orator. The city of Seattle was named after him . . . well, almost. Neither the spelling error nor the altered pronunciation upset Chief Sealth. He was, in fact, quite pleased that the great city was called Seattle and not Sealth. In Indian culture, it is believed that after your body is dead you will roll over in your grave at every mention of your name. I'm pretty sure that Chief Sealth was pleased to know that he was not destined to spend eternity spinning on the other side.

4 | Chinook Jargon

IN THE 1830's, PRESIDENT MADISON SIGNED THE MADISON DOCTRINE declaring that everything west of the Mississippi was Indian country. By 1872 all of the Indians from the Atlantic to the Pacific were living on reservations. Treaties were signed . . . people shook hands and gave their word. Certain promises were made to the Indians in exchange for their signing over all of their rights to the land that they had occupied for countless generations. There is still considerable disagreement between the United States government and the Indian tribes regarding the interpretation of those treaties. What did my ancestors believe they were agreeing to when they put their mark on the treaty paper? How could my people and the government possibly have such different interpretations of the provisions outlined in the treaties?

Grandpa Benny George was a S'Klallam Indian from the Port Gamble Reservation near the town of Hansville. Grandma Martha was a Suquamish Indian. She lived on the Port Madison Indian Reservation. The Port Madison Reservation was an easy two-hour horse ride down the trail from the Port Gamble S'Klallam Tribe.

Benny and Martha met by chance in the woods one day, and they fell in love. Grandma was a devout Catholic, and Grandpa was a confirmed atheist. And as such things go, their wedding ceremony was held in the Suquamish Roman Catholic Church and was never an issue for discussion. They made their home on Grandma's property in Suquamish, and there they raised a family.

Grandpa Benny dug clams, fished, logged, and picked brush for subsistence. Grandma was an oyster shucker at the oyster plant in downtown Suquamish. She was very good at it, and at public gatherings she would often draw an admiring crowd. At potlatches, money would be wagered on whether or not my grandma could shuck a five-gallon bucket of oysters in a given period of time. Her nimble fingers could spin an oyster apart in the blink of an eye, and betting against her would get you excellent odds but very few victories.

Grandma never was much for driving. She left that distasteful and tedious business to her husband. Grandpa owned an old, rusty, Ford pickup truck that had served him well for many years. The shocks were well worn from too many back-road potholes, and the bed had seen everything from fresh salmon to gutted and quartered elk. Grandpa was at one with his truck. He swore that old truck would drive its way home as straight as the trickster-crow flies, even after he had consumed an entire fifth of whiskey.

Seems as though Grandma was not all that comfortable with Grandpa driving inebriated, especially when he claimed that his truck ran on autopilot. So, when I was old enough to drive, I would swing by my grandparents' house in the morning to pick up Grandma and take her down to the plant. I always entered the house through the back door, which was never locked. Grandma was usually at the stove cooking breakfast, and Grandpa would be sitting at his place by the table carving on a piece of wood, or running a pipe cleaner through his pipe, or working on any one of a dozen or so other maintenance tasks. I always sat at my place at the table, in the same corner, and in the same chair that I had sat in as a young boy. I spent countless hours sitting in that chair, watching my grandpa work. His fingers were bent and twisted with age, and his hands were leathered and scarred; yet, I was always amazed by his skill, dexterity and craftsmanship.

My grandma never let anyone leave her table with an empty stomach. She was a wonderful cook. Her pastries and oven-baked bread were legendary, and they seldom saw a second day. On this particular morning, Grandma poured me a cup of coffee from the percolator and slid a heaping stack of hotcakes under my chin. In front of me were three or four different topping choices of her homemade jellies and preserves, and while I feasted, Grandma and Grandpa discussed the day's events in their native tongues.

Like a lot of people who are married for many years, my grandparents argued constantly, but the exchanges were usually good-natured and their affection for each other was always very evident. Grandpa was quite fond of complaining about all that ailed him. He usually had some reminiscent commentary on the sad state of current affairs and how things had been much different when he was a boy.

"We had to walk to school every day in the snow," he proclaimed in his native dialect, "in our bare feet, uphill both ways."

He made the sign of a long journey with his hand and then laughed out loud. "You can't remember that long ago!"

Grandma countered, chuckling to herself.

Grandpa ignored her fussing as if she weren't there and continued complaining, "That darn cow got out again last night," he said, "and broke down the fence."

Grandma would turn and shake the spatula at him, scolding, "You old fool, you just said that the cow got out and ran across the water."

There were several seconds of silence, and then the three of us laughed aloud at the humor of it.

These mixed-up exchanges between my grandparents were not uncommon and were often the source of good-natured ribbing. As I said, the Port Gamble S'Klallam Tribe was right up the road, no more than eight miles from the Port Madison Indian Reservation. It was easy walking distance and yet the two Indian dialects, similar enough that many words were the same, were different enough that the S'Klallam word for water may have meant cow in Suquamish and cow may have meant fence.

When the Whites first came to the Northwest, they trapped beaver and otter for a living. There were wealthy folks back East and in Europe that were eager to pay top dollar for furs. The trappers sold their catch to the fur companies. The fur companies sold to the furriers who crafted beautiful garments from the skins.

The Indians had many commodities that were relished by the White trappers: roots and berries for food and medicine, clams and oysters, as well as fresh and smoked salmon. The White trappers had commodities that were relished by the Indians: pots and pans, guns and shells, and of course, alcohol. The White trappers depended on particular goods from the Indians and vice versa, so it was quite natural that some form of trading evolved. The Whites bartered with all of the tribes living along the inland coastal waters of the Puget Sound; however, the different Indian dialects proved to be a major disadvantage when conducting business, and it was virtually impossible to master them all. What evolved, out of necessity, was a basic 300-word vocabulary that was understood by traders and Indians alike. This crude language came to be called Chinook Jargon, and it worked very well for commerce, becoming the accepted form of communication during barter and trade.

5 | Manifest Destiny

WAVE AFTER WAVE OF WHITE SETTLERS FOLLOWED THE TRADERS AND trappers into the new territory. This place was a paradise. Huge coniferous forests blanketed the hills and valleys. Trees were six to twelve feet in diameter and hundreds of years old. The Puget Sound itself was a sparkling clean, inland sea of unprecedented beauty. You could stand on the shore and see eagle and seabird, whale and sea lion. In the late fall, spawning salmon would plug the lower stretches of every river and stream And after the salmon had laid their eggs, the riverbanks would be covered with the carcasses of thousands of fish. Their rotting bodies would fill the river with nutrients upon which the young salmon would feast and grow strong, and the amazing cycle of life and sacrifice would begin anew.

To the Indians, the land provided subsistence. The woods literally teemed with beaver, bear, deer and elk. Eagles soared over the treetops. Songbirds filled the air with beautiful music. Fresh, clear, cold water from mountain springs and glaciers tumbled down from the hills and meandered through the lowlands and out to sea.

To the Whites, the forests meant instant wealth. The city of Seattle was expanding at a steady rate, and millions of acres of virgin timber fueled the growth. Seattle was a boomtown that offered opportunity and a fresh start for many young families. The air was clean and the water pure, and the game and seafood plentiful. Seattle became a vibrant seaport. Goods were shipped northward from San Francisco in exchange for salmon and lumber. Thousands upon thousands of men, young and old, from all corners of the world, lined the downtown piers and docks awaiting a boat ride to the gold fields in Alaska.

Acre after acre of ancient, virgin forest fell to the woodsman's axe as town after town sprung up across the countryside. There was an insatiable need for food and fire, farm and fish, and Mother Nature's bounty seemed endless. Entire communities . . . schools, businesses, and churches . . . sprung up overnight on the shores of Puget Sound, while the flow of Whites to the new territory continued unchecked. It soon became apparent that more pristine waterfront property would be needed to make room for new towns and settlements. Unfortunately, the Indians were occupying way too much prime real estate. The settlers gathered in their town halls and churches, on the streets, and in their taverns. Beneath the patriotic banner of manifest destiny, and the irresistible lure of wealth, the citizenry arrived at a general consensus . . . something had to be done about the bothersome Indians.

6 | Word of Honor

THE GOOD CITIZENS PETITIONED THE FEDERAL GOVERNMENT FOR action. The Federal Government proposed a plan. The plan was hardly original. It was the same plan used over and over again as the tidal wave of Whites moved westward across the continent. The Indians fought for their way of life, but the Whites were many and their weapons superior. Though the Indians occasionally found victory in battle, nothing could alter their destiny.

The Federal Government called together the Puget Sound tribes in 1855 for the signing of the Point Elliot Treaty. Chief Sealth, representing the Federation of Tribes, acted as the principal signer. The Indian leaders came to Point Elliot from the area between the Puyallup River and the Canadian border and included, from south to north, the Duwamish, Suquamish, Snoqualmie, Snohomish, Stillaguamish, Swinomish, Skagits, and Lummis.

The treaty promised the Indians that they would be given land that would always be theirs . . . land that they could call their own . . . the government would own it, but it was theirs. The treaty promised to provide educational benefits and health care. The treaty also promised harvesting rights on their usual and accustomed hunting grounds.

All of these promises were made in exchange for ceding all rights to thousands of acres of pristine territory . . . territory that had provided the Indians with subsistence for countless generations. The Federal Government promised that for each acre the Indians ceded, or signed over to the government, a fee of ten cents would be paid . . . ten acres for a buck! The Indians were unable to comprehend an offer of money in exchange for land. To the Indians the land, like the wind, the sun, or the seasons, was not something that could be owned. The land had always been and would always be. Congress ratified the treaties, but the money was never appropriated.

During the proceedings, Chief Sealth recited the following speech, which has been interpreted by many Whites as one of the greatest statements ever made concerning the relationship between a people and the earth. I would not disagree; however, I also hear great sadness and reluctant capitulation . . . these are the words of a proud and intelligent man who had witnessed, in his lifetime, the destruction of all that his people held sacred. To me, his words ring with anger. He had seen the White man take everything and give nothing back. Could it be that his speech is a warning . . . a vision . . . a premonition . . . that the White man is destined to die in his own waste. I wonder.

CHIEF SEALTH'S SPEECH

Yonder sky that has wept tears of compassion
upon our fathers for centuries untold,
and which to us looks eternal, may change.
Today is fair,
tomorrow may be overcast with clouds.

My words are like the stars that never set.
What Seattle says the Great Chief at Washington can rely upon
with as much certainty as our paleface brothers can rely upon
the return of the seasons.

The son of the White Chief says
his father sends us greetings of friendship and good will.
This is kind,
for we know he has little need of our friendship in return
because his people are many.
They are like the grass that covers the vast prairies,
while my people are few
and resemble the scattering trees of a storm-swept plain.

The Great, and I presume, also good,
White Chief sends us word that he wants to buy our lands
but is willing to allow us
to reserve enough to live on comfortably.
This indeed appears generous,
for the Red man no longer has rights that he need respect,
and the offer may be wise, also
for we are no longer in need of a great country.

There was a time when our people covered the whole land
as the waves of a wind-ruffled sea covers its shell-paved floor.
But the time has long since passed away
with the greatness of tribes now almost forgotten.

I will not mourn over our untimely decay,
nor reproach my paleface brothers for hastening it,
for we, too,
may have been somewhat to blame.

When our young men grow angry
at some real or imaginary wrong,
and disfigure their faces with black paint,
their hearts, also, are disfigured and turn black,
and then their cruelty is relentless and knows no bounds,
and our old men are not able to restrain them.

But let us hope that hostilities
between the Red man and his paleface brothers
may never return.
We would have everything to lose and nothing to gain.

True it is, that revenge,
with our young braves is considered gain,
even at the cost of their own lives,

but old men who stay at home in times of war,
and mothers who have sons to lose,
know better.

Our great father, Washington,
for I presume he is now our father as well as yours,
since George has moved his boundaries to the North
our great and good father, I say,
sends us word by his son,
who, no doubt, is a great chief among his people
that if we do as he desires he will protect us.

His brave armies will be to us a bristling wall of strength,
and his great ships of war will fill our harbors
So that our ancient enemies far to the northward
the Simsiams and Hyas,
will no longer frighten our women and old men.
Then he will be our father
and we will be his children.

But can that ever be?
Your God is not our God!
Your God loves your people and hates mine!
He folds his strong arm lovingly around the White man
and leads him as a father leads his infant son
but He has forsaken his Red children,
He makes your people wax strong every day
and soon they will fill all the land;
while my people are ebbing away
like a fast receding tide that will never flow again.
The White man's God cannot love his Red children
or he would protect them.
They seem to be orphans who can look nowhere for help.

How then can we become brothers?
How can your Father become our Father
and bring us prosperity,
and awaken in us dreams of returning greatness?

Your God seems to us to be partial.
He came to the White man.
We never saw Him, never heard His voice.
He gave the White man laws,
but had no word for His Red children
whose teeming millions once filled this vast continent
as the stars fill the firmament.

No. We are two distinct races,
and must remain ever so,
there is little common between us.

The ashes of our ancestors are sacred
and their final resting-place is hallowed ground,
while you wander away from the tombs of your fathers
seemingly without regrets.

Your religion was written on tablets of stone
by the iron finger of an angry God,
lest you might forget it.
The Red man could never remember nor comprehend it.

Our religion is the traditions of our ancestors
the dreams of our old men,
given to them by the Great Spirit,
and the visions of our Sachems,
and is written in the hearts of our people.

Your dead cease to love you

and the homes of their nativity
as soon as they pass the portals of the tomb.
They wander far away beyond the stars,
are soon forgotten and never return.

Our dead never forget the beautiful world
that gave them being.
They still love its winding rivers,
its great mountains and its sequestered vales,
and they ever yearn in tenderest affection
over the lonely-hearted living,
and often return to visit and comfort them.

Day and night cannot dwell together.
The Red man has ever fled the approach of the White man,
as the changing mist on the mountain side
flees before the blazing morning sun.

However, your proposition seems a just one,
and I think my folks will accept it
and will retire to the reservation you offer them,
and will dwell apart and in peace,
for the words of the Great White Chief
seem to be the voice of Nature speaking to my people
out of the thick darkness that is fast gathering around them
like a dense fog floating inward from a midnight sea.

It matters little where we pass the remainder of our days.
They are not many.
The Indian's night promises to be dark.
No bright star hovers above his horizon.
Some grim Nemesis of our race is on the Red man's trail,
and wherever he goes he will hear
the sure approaching footsteps of the fell destroyer

and prepare to meet his doom,
as does the wounded doe
that hears the approaching footsteps of the hunter.

A few more moons, a few more winters,
and not one of all the mighty hosts
that once filled this broad land
or that now roam in fragmentary bands
through these vast solitudes or lived in happy homes,
protected by the Great Spirit,
will remain to weep over the graves of a people
once as powerful and as hopeful as your own!

But why should I repine?
Why should I murmur at the fate of my people?
Tribes are made up of individuals
and are no better than they.
Men come and go like the waves of a sea.
A tear, a tamanamus, a dirge
and they are gone from our longing eyes forever.
Even the White man, whose God walked and talked
with him as friend to friend,
is not exempt from the common destiny.
We may be brothers after all.
We shall see.

We will ponder your proposition,
and when we have decided we will tell you.
But should we accept it,
I here and now make this first condition,
that we will not be denied the privilege,
without molestation,
of visiting the graves of our ancestors and friends.

Every part of this country is sacred to my people.
Every hillside, every valley, every plain and grove
has been hallowed by some fond memory
or some sad experience of my tribe.
Even the rocks,
which seem to lie dumb as they swelter in the sun
along the silent shore in solemn grandeur

thrill with memories of past events
connected with the fate of my people,
the very dust under your feet
responds more lovingly to our footsteps than to yours,
because it is the ashes of our ancestors,
and our bare feet are conscious of the sympathetic touch,
for the soil is rich with the life of our kindred.

The sable braves,
and fond mothers,
and glad-hearted maidens,
and the little children who lived and rejoiced here
and whose very names are now forgotten,
still love these solitudes
and their deep fastnesses eventide grow shadowy
with the presence of dusky spirits.

and when the last Red man
shall have perished from the earth
and his memory among White men
shall have become a myth,
these shores will swarm with the invisible dead of my tribe
and when your children's children shall think themselves alone
in the field, the store, the shop, upon the highway,
or in the silence of the woods,
they will not be alone.
In all the earth there is no place dedicated to solitude.

At night, when the streets of your cities and villages
shall be silent and you think them deserted,
they will throng with the returning hosts
that once filled and still love this beautiful land.
The White man will never be alone.
Let him be just and deal kindly with my people,
for the dead are not powerless.

———

This story was passed down to me through the generations as I have passed it down to my children. The Point Elliot Treaty was read to an interpreter who translated the English text into Chinook Jargon. I have been asked on many occasions to speak to groups in the community on the subject of Indian history and culture. It is very important to me that, after my presentation, the audience is left with a better understanding of the Indian perspective. I have developed an exercise that I believe serves that purpose.

Standing in front of a group, I will ask for a show of hands from anyone in the audience who can fluently speak a foreign language. Several hands will inevitably go up. I will pick one of those folks, tell them that I'd like to borrow them for a minute and invite them up front with me. The last time I did this exercise a guy named Bob raised his hand and claimed to fluently speak Spanish. I invited Bob to the front of the room. I then asked for a volunteer who spoke just a little Spanish. Several more hands went up. I picked a young lady named Michelle and asked her if she would please join Bob and me for a little demonstration.

I asked Bob to stand on my left and face the group, and I asked Michelle to stand on my right. I pulled a 3 x 5 card from my shirt pocket. On the card I had written the following words in English:

You can only buy Big Macs with cheese and no onions on Tuesdays. You must have my permission to go buy milk. You cannot leave this area without first asking my permission and it will cost you $2.00 every time you go.

I gave the card to Bob and asked him to look it over and then translate the words into Spanish and read the card to Michelle. I told Michelle to listen carefully to the Spanish Bob was reading and then translate what she heard back into English for the audience. Bob read the card to Michelle.

"Puedes comprar unicamente Big Macs con queso y sin cebollas Los Martes. Debes tener mi permiso para comprar leche no te puedos ir de esta area sin permiso mio y te costava $2 cada vez que vayas."

After asking Bob to repeat the message several times, Michelle did her very best to decipher Bob's fluent Spanish. She translated the message into English, which she shared with the crowd. Her translation left much to be desired.

"We buy Big Macs and something on Tuesdays to have permission for to buy milk. I have $2.00 only to spend."

I then read the real message to the audience. Everyone had a good laugh. I explained that when Chief Sealth gathered the chiefs and leaders of the Puget Sound tribes together for the signing of the Point Elliot Treaty that they were asked to make their mark on the paper to signify that they were in agreement with the provisions as outlined in the treaty. The Government Man read the treaty in English to an interpreter who translated the Government Man's word into the 300-word Chinook Jargon language. So, what did the tribal leaders hear from the English treaty paper to the interpreter to Chinook Jargon to their individual dialects? To this day, that is a bone of contention among the Whites and Indians . . . what are our treaty rights and what do they really mean?

In 1982, the Suquamish tribe filed a lawsuit for ownership of eleven miles of tidelands. This stretch of beach was where, in our communal way of life, our ancestors had migrated and gathered shellfish for subsistence. The eleven miles of tidelands was ceded land. The Federal Government, in their infinite wisdom, did not include tidelands at the making of the treaties, though that was the interpretation of the tribe based on the way the provisions of the treaty were presented through Chinook Jargon.

I was asked by the tribe to be a spokesman . . . to go out into the Suquamish community and explain the tribe's point of view. We had a community gathering at the little brown church across from the football field. Some of the most outspoken non-Indian folks showed up for that meeting. Many were members of U.P.O.W. (Upland Property Owners of Washington) who garnered Senator Slade Gorton's support regarding tribal rites and issues. I feared for my life in that meeting. A prominent member of the School Board, also anti-Indian, attended that meeting. Her house was right next to the Tribal Center . . . medium-bank waterfront property, so that speaks of the money itself.

After the meeting, I specifically invited several of the most outspoken folks to my house. I had a nice home on 2½ acres off the reservation. I opened my house to them. The house smelled of fresh coffee and fresh baked cookies. I thought it was important to break the stereotype . . . to leave the impression that maybe there are some Indians who do have some knowledge . . . that do have some energy and some sense of pride in what they have and what they do.

I had two reasons for hosting that meeting. I wanted to convey our point of view to these folks . . . to open their eyes and their ears enough to see and hear what the Suquamish people were doing. I also wanted to know why they felt the way they did. I was challenged by our Tribal Council and our legal staff not to invite those folks to the table, and yet I knew that these were the people whom I must talk to. I intended to meet with them, with or without the tribe's approval.

One of my apprentice instructors taught me the importance of knowing your enemy . . . that you must go to the heart of the opposition's camp and try to understand exactly where they sit, where they come from, and why they think the way they do. Perhaps then you can find some kind of common ground . . . a deeper understanding. That is why I invited the leadership of the opposition's camp into my house. I had no hidden agenda. I was just searching for an understanding. Quite frankly, I was surprised they showed up. They accepted my hospitality. I hoped it was out of respect, because we all knew each other growing up.

We ate cookies and drank coffee. I listened to their fears and their concerns. They listened to what I had to say, and they listened to what our legal staff had to say. Their minds could not be changed. At the end of the meeting, the two sides could not be moved off dead center with a stick of dynamite. We finally had our day in court, and the tribe lost the tideland issue. The court upheld their interpretation of the treaty.

7 | Assimilation

AFTER THE SIGNING OF THE POINT ELLIOT TREATY, THE NORTHWEST Indian Tribes were moved on to their respective reservations. The United States Government established the Bureau of Indian Affairs to watch over the Indians. The Bureau of Indian Affairs assigned White agents to each reservation as caretakers of the natives . . . to help them adapt to their new role in the White man's world. In many cases these agents were elbow-deep in graft and corruption. They made sure that the local bathtub and toilet salesmen were awarded lucrative contracts to install bathtubs and toilets in Indian houses where there was no indoor plumbing.

The Bureau concluded that, in order to bring moral and religious advancement to the heathens, they must assimilate the ignorant natives into the White man's culture. God was called in. Religious associations and missionary societies took control of local Indian agencies, and the reservations were divided up among the major Christian religions. The Suquamish were assigned to the Roman Catholics along with the Tulalip, Swinomish, and Lummi tribes. The Makah were offered up to the Christian Union and then later to the Methodists, who were already firmly entrenched on the Quinault Reservation. The Skokomish Agency consolidated with the Puyallup Agency, and they were placed under the guiding light of the Congressional Church.

> *Your religion was written on tablets of stone*
> *by the iron finger of an angry God,*
> *lest you might forget it.*
> *The Red man could never remember nor comprehend it.*
> *Our religion is the traditions of our ancestors*

the dreams of our old men,
given to them by the Great Spirit,
and the visions of our Sachems,
and is written in the hearts of our people.

Indians across the country were systematically indoctrinated. Churches popped up on every reservation. It was deemed unacceptable for the aborigines to believe in non-Christian values and ethics. Indian children were taken from their homes and placed in Christian Boarding Schools. They were dressed as Whites and instructed on how to behave as Whites. Their hair was cut, and they were taught to fluently read and write the English language.

I remember my grandpa telling me stories of Uncle Webster. Web was our Tribal Council Chairman for many years. The church put him in a boarding school as a young boy. I have numerous aunts and uncles who spent their young lives in boarding schools. Web, like the other Indian children, was eager to fit in . . . to be like the Whites. My grandpa told me about Web trying to scrub the pigment from his face. He rubbed raw sores on his skin trying to look White.

Proud Indian warriors became tillers of the land and herders of cattle. Our culture was taboo. Our ceremonies were unacceptable. Our religious and spiritual beliefs were labeled heresy.

But can that ever be?
Your God is not our God!
Your God loves your people and hates mine!
He folds his strong arm lovingly around the White man
and leads him as a father leads his infant son
but He has forsaken his Red children,
He makes your people wax strong every day
and soon they will fill all the land;
while my people are ebbing away
like a fast receding tide that will never flow again.
The White man's God cannot love his Red children
or he would protect them.
They seem to be orphans who can look nowhere for help.

How then can we become brothers?
How can your Father become our Father
and bring us prosperity,
and awaken in us dreams of returning greatness?

Your God seems to us to be partial.
He came to the White man.
We never saw Him, never heard His voice.
He gave the White man laws,
but had no word for His Red children
whose teeming millions once filled this vast continent
as the stars fill the firmament.

To ensure a smooth transition, free from organized resistance, the Indians were sedated with alcohol. Every man, woman, and child was allotted 150 gallons of whiskey per year. This is a matter of historical fact. An Indian agent for the Congressional Church was pleased to note that the Indians on the Skokomish Reservation seemed to be adapting well. They had adjusted to the practical elements of White civilization. They had built comfortable houses, barns, woodsheds and outhouses, and had set out small orchards. They had gathered around them the substantial comforts of civilized life. Indoors, their floors were smooth . . . the rooms were warmed with fireplaces. Their food was cooked on stoves and eaten on tables with knives and forks on plates and dishes as White people do. They had bedsteads with feather beds, sheets and pillowcases, as well as clocks and looking glasses, and they kept their persons as neat as a large majority of the White people living on the frontiers.

Many non-Indians today ask why Indians still receive funding from the Federal Government. I ask why we have never received the money as promised by treaty for the land that we were forced to surrender to the Government. I ask why we were never provided with the educational and health benefits as promised by treaty. Congress ratified the treaties but the money was never appropriated.

Many non-Indians today question why Indians have special fishing privileges and the right to harvest shellfish on private property. I question why the Suquamish Tribe lost the lawsuit that would have allowed tribal members to harvest shellfish on eleven miles of local beaches where our forefathers foraged for subsistence for a millennium.

Many non-Indians still believe that the Indians should just be absorbed into White society . . . assimilated . . . that it would be best to just forget the past and look forward to the future. I say that assimilation—taking away the religious and cultural beliefs of our people—has left nothing but a shell . . . a spiritless, dysfunctional shell. I say that Indians do not wish to be Whites or Blacks or Asians or Hispanics . . . we simply wish to be Indians, and I worry that, if we forget the past, we are surely destined to relive it.

8 | **From the Stump to the Tree**

LOUISA PETERS WAS AN ELDERLY SUQUAMISH WOMAN. SHE WAS THE daughter of one of the original Indians who were allotted land on the newly established Port Madison Indian Reservation. The Government Man told all of the Indians, including Louisa's parents that "This land is set aside for you by the signing of the Point Elliot Treaty. When you put your mark on the paper, this is what you agree to. This is your property on your reservation . . . it's got your name on it. The government owns it . . . but it's yours."

> *The Great, and I presume, also good,*
> *White Chief sends us word that he wants to buy our lands*
> *but is willing to allow us*
> *to reserve enough to live on comfortably.*
> *This indeed appears generous,*
> *for the Red man no longer has rights that he need respect,*
> *and the offer may be wise, also*
> *for we are no longer in need of a great country.*

Louisa Peters lived her entire life on the reservation in the house her father had built on his allotted one hundred and forty acres. Louisa inherited that property when her parents died. She had seen ninety-three summers and was in poor health.

When Grandma Martha was a young girl, she and another young girl, Mary

Adams, looked after Louisa when she became ill. They loved the old woman. She had a kind heart and a gentle spirit, and she was very wise. Martha and Mary lovingly called her Grandma Louisa. They sought her out for counsel, and she always had time to listen to their problems and to offer sound advice.

Martha and Mary would come over to Grandma Louisa's house every day after school. They did the dishes and swept the floor and cooked her dinner, but their real gift to Louisa was their company. Louisa was very lonely. Her husband had died many years before, and she was never able to have children. Her good friends had long since passed, and her neighbors no longer bothered to visit. Since she had become ill, she was unable to get out on her own. The daily visits from Mary and my grandma were a Godsend for the old woman, and a great bond of love and friendship united the three of them.

One day Louisa asked Martha and Mary to assist her in getting up from her chair. They helped her rise and supported her arms as she walked toward the front door, slowly moving one foot before the other. At her request they helped her out on the porch, down the stairs, and into the yard. She paused several times to catch her breath. The sun was high in the sky, and Louisa closed her eyes and smiled. The wild flowers were in bloom, and she breathed in the sweet fragrance. The warm sun on her face sent a shiver through her body. In her mind she was once again a young girl running and skipping with boundless energy.

"Are you all right?" Mary asked.

Louisa opened her eyes, awakened from her dream, and smiled at the two girls.

"I am fine," she replied. "I was just remembering things that were long ago and are now long gone."

Louisa took several steps forward on her own, and the two girls stepped back as if they could sense her need for privacy. She gazed upon the land that had been a part of her for so many seasons. She thought of her father and how he would dry the salmon on the racks behind the house and how he would take her hand when she was a young girl and walk with her down to the bay. She thought of how her mother would bake sweet cakes on the hot rocks in the fire pit and softly sing old Indian songs to her at night to help her find sleep. She thought of the young men who came to court and how her father would question them as to their intentions. She remembered how wonderful it was when she fell in love and how she still ached for her husband's touch.

"Grandma Louisa. Is there something we can do?" Martha asked, hesitantly, unsure if she should interrupt.

Louisa said nothing but raised both hands and beckoned the two girls to her side. As they stood by her, Louisa pointed to a large, old-growth stump in the corner of the garden. "My father cut down that tree when he built this house. It took him many days."

Louisa looked at Mary. There was a tear in the old woman's eye. "From this stump," she said, "to that tree." She pointed to a tall cedar tree on the far side of her property and drew a line with the motion of her hand. "This," she said, sweeping her hand to the right, "this land I gift to you, Mary, and this," she said, sweeping her hand to the left, "this land I gift to you, Martha. When I pass, I will be as the line between the stump and the tree, and the two of you will always be at my side."

There was nothing more said that day, for there was nothing more to say. Louisa crossed over shortly thereafter. Mary and Martha were gifted the property and shared a common boundary . . . the line between the stump and the tree . . . and this they knew to be true.

9 | The One-eyed Chilean

SEATTLE WAS A THRIVING SEAPORT IN THE EARLY PART OF THE TWEN-tieth century. Ships from all corners of the world brought their goods through the Strait of Juan de Fuca and down to Seattle.

One day a Chilean freighter was pier side in Seattle, unloading its cargo in preparation to take on a consignment of goods. One of the Chilean deck hands jumped ship. He made his way down the pier and hopped a small boat that was part of the mosquito fleet bound for the Kitsap Peninsula. There, he found work as a laborer at one of the many sawmills that dotted the countryside.

He spoke no English, so the other mill hands called him Ambrose because it sounded similar enough to his Chilean name and Andrews after the owner of the mill. Ambrose Andrews earned extra spending money picking brush in the woods, and it was on one of these jobs that he met Mary Adams. Mary was quite smitten with the young, dark, and mysterious Chilean. The two of them, though they were never wed, were inseparable, and Ambrose eventually moved in with Mary on her property in Suquamish . . . just to the right of the line between the stump and the tree. They lived together for many years and became common-law husband and wife.

Now Ambrose, it seems, was quite fond of seafood. He especially liked Dunge-ness crab and the numerous shellfish that were there on the beach for the taking. One day, while digging a bucket full of clams, he was squirted in the eye. The eye became infected and Ambrose, who was not known for being the brightest bulb on the tree, failed to seek proper medical attention. By the time he went to the doctor it was too late and he lost his eye.

Ambrose was a great mystery to many. He was an anomaly . . . an Indian from Chile, thousands of miles from home, with no history and no past. The Suquamish tribe took him in. They called him, with all good humor, "Amby the One-eyed Chilean," and Amby considered the name a small price to pay for their acceptance. Unfortunately, and unbeknownst to Mary and Martha, Amby developed a nasty habit.

Amby the One-eyed Chilean used to take long walks through the woods. He would look for those little pie-plate survey markers that are used in a square world to identify the location of property boundaries. Amby deduced that since the pie plates represented lines of ownership, then moving the pie plates would be a simple way to increase the size of his property. So, Amby would simply pry the pie plates loose and transplant them to wherever he wanted his new property line to be.

Everything went along famously for Amby and his traveling boundary markers until Mary Adams became ill and died. Amby, being Mary's common-law husband, inherited all of her tribal property to the right of the line between the stump and the tree. Mary's tribal property was United States Government Trust Status property, held in trust by the government for the enrolled tribal members on the reservation, gifted to her by Louisa Peters. Suddenly it was reverted to Fee Status property when inherited by one Ambrose Andrews, a non-Suquamish, one-eyed Chilean who had jumped ship.

Amby found himself right smack dab in the middle of the American Dream . . . he was the sole owner of acres of valuable, pristine, land-locked, no-bank waterfront. The change from Trust to Fee Status property also entitled this once poor Chilean immigrant to experience yet another special privilege afforded all landowning Americans. The IRS abruptly notified Amby that since his inherited land was now Fee Status property and no longer held in trust that he owed Uncle Sam a considerable amount of property taxes, and they were payable immediately. Amby had no cash. He was property rich and cash poor, and there was no way he could afford to pay taxes.

Amby figured he would simply sell off the property to pay the taxes. So, he hooked up with a shyster attorney from Poulsbo. This attorney convinced Amby to divide Mary's land into nine separate segments of pristine, no-bank waterfront. Amby then proceeded to sell the nine lots eleven times to wealthy White folks. The families that purchased the lots in the middle were quite satisfied with their acquisitions; however, the families that purchased lots number ten and eleven, the two lots that didn't actually exist, were not happy. The folks who bought the lot right next to my grandma's property immediately contacted an attorney who informed my grandma that his clients had just acquired sixty feet of her property.

My grandma immediately protested. She told the attorney that she had been gifted all of the property to the left of the line between the stump and the tree. The attorney told my grandma that the pie-plate boundary markers were located sixty feet inside her property line and that those boundary markers were the legal location of the property line.

My grandma was very confused. She did not understand government lot lines or survey markers or other such things. Her understanding was rooted in something far more tangible than the White man's measurements. Grandma knew that she and Mary Adams had shared the life and the love and the memory of Grandma Peters, and they were forever bonded by the line between the stump and the tree. This she knew to be true.

My grandma asked the family for help. I knew that Mary and my grandma knew nothing of today's modern surveyor who shoots the sun and the moon. They had no concept of global positioning satellite technology that can pinpoint your location on the planet earth within inches. That a government lot is not a full forty-acre section had little to do with the bond between Grandma Martha, Mary, and Louisa Peters. Martha and Mary lived their entire adult lives bonded by a gift from an old woman's heart. What they knew was a very simple and very basic truth. They were each gifted a portion of land and entrusted to take care of it unto death and, in turn, gift it down to their descendants.

Grandma had a herd of cows that ran free over the entire two hundred acres. The boundary was never disputed. She put up a fence in 1946 to contain her livestock. Grandma directed the folks who were building her fence to hold it in two feet on her side just to be sure there would be no problems with Mary. Mary was very alive and well at the time and she did not contest that fence.

My dad and I, along with a couple of cousins, went to Sand Point and found a copy of the 1853 Van Clief survey . . . the survey that established the original boundaries of the Port Madison Indian Reservation. We discovered that the surveyors for the Van Clief Company laid out the reservation without triangulating back, as was customary, to ensure that the segments were square. Some of the lots were actually trapezoidal.

The law says that the oldest survey takes precedence. We contacted the Bureau of Land Management and asked their experts to help us sort this mess out. With information from the 1853 survey, and using modern surveying techniques, it was determined that we were actually encroaching thirty feet instead of sixty feet.

I protested. "Let's talk about the line between the stump and the tree," I said. "Let's talk about three ladies who didn't understand leaps and bounds and proper surveying techniques. Let's talk about the wishes of Louisa Peters when she gifted the land to Martha and Mary. There must be some kind of unspoken law that would allow us to honor the wishes of those three ladies?"

I contacted the Bureau of Indian Affairs for help. I sent them videotapes to explain the situation. I told them that the dying wish of Louisa Peters was in direct conflict with a government survey that neglected to triangulate back to the starting point to verify that the sections they surveyed were square. I explained about Amby the One-eyed Chilean arbitrarily moving boundary markers. They did nothing. We got no action from the Bureau of Indian Affairs, nothing . . . a complete dereliction of duty.

My grandma passed over while all of this was going on. In her will, she gifted a portion of her property to me the same way Louisa Peters had gifted the property to her. I am responsible to protect that property . . . it's mine to take care of. The government has the title and I have the deed.

My uncle, through the luck of the draw, was gifted the disputed portion of Grandma's property. Half of his house stands on the property in contention. His daughter is a retired Ma Bell employee from Chicago. She and her husband had more money than they knew what to do with. When they were divorced, they sold off all of their assets and divvied up the cash. She brought her Chicago money home and dumped thousands and thousands of dollars into court costs and attorney fees and was finally able to buy justice. The property line was returned to where Louisa Peters meant it to be . . . on the line between the stump and the tree.

I built a house down by water on the portion of land that was gifted to me. I know the exact location of every board and every nail. My sons worked with me, side by side. There is enough property there for all three of my children, and one day I will gift it down to them the way it was gifted down to me. They can build their houses around us if they'd like. I have another piece of property that I've already divided amongst them. I don't think that any of my kids will ever move back to the reservation because of their exposure to my involvement with tribal government. I doubt that they will ever want to live there. It angers me. If they choose to gift the property to their children, that would be good, and I hope that they do. I really hope that they do.

10 | Uncle Louie, Benny, Ted, and Cees

BASEBALL WAS ENTERTAINMENT ON THE SUQUAMISH RESERVATION
. . . the great Native American pastime. Every Friday and Saturday night during the
spring and summer, weather permitting, there would be a hardball game in
progress on the downtown ball field.

Other tribes would show up in town, and the hills and bleachers would fill with
fans. Some of the rivalries were decades old and the entire show was fueled by an
endless supply of whiskey.

I attended most of the games with my dad. He always insisted that we sit on top
of the hill. "Let's sit up here, boys," he would say. "If we go down on the field, they'll
make me umpire the damn game." I think Dad just wanted to take a pull or two
and be left alone.

There were no official uniforms or organized tournaments. It was just baseball
. . . sandlot baseball . . . a chance for friends and relatives to get together and play.
When there was no visiting tribe, it was customary for the downtown, wealthy,
waterfront boys to mix it up with the hard living, whiskey drinking, uptown boys,
though I must say, it was always in good fun . . . it was the joy of the game that
mattered.

Great-uncle Louie George was an excellent athlete. Many people have said that
he was the Jim Thorpe of the Suquamish. Uncle Louie was a right-handed pitcher.
He could hurl the cowhide upwards of ninety-five miles per hour. He had a wicked
curve ball that went straight for the batter's head, only to break at the last second

and snap into the catcher's mitt for a strike.

There were many semi-pro baseball teams in Seattle back then that were willing to pay good money for Uncle Louie's arm. Louie kept a uniform from every team packed in his trunk. He would ride the mosquito fleet to the big city and go from ballpark to ballpark, pitching for the team that offered him the biggest paycheck.

One year a local promoter offered to take the Suquamish baseball team to Japan. The Suquamish tribe fielded one hell of a ball club in the twenties and thirties. The team included Uncle Louie, my grandfather, and Web, the guy who tried to wash the color from his face. There is a picture of that baseball team on the wall in the reception area of the Suquamish Tribal Center.

When the team arrived in Japan, they were already scheduled to play several Japanese teams. Baseball was very big in Japan, and the novelty of an Indian and Japanese ballgame guaranteed a large draw. Louie was the starting pitcher in the first game. Thousands of Japanese fans filled the stands.

Uncle Louie took the mound in the bottom of the first inning. The first batter came up to the plate, and Louie pitched the count full. He got the sign from our catcher to hurl his famous curve. He went into motion and released the ball. The Japanese player saw the ball heading straight for his head and instead of ducking backwards he went forward. The ball curved right into his temple and dropped him . . . dead on the spot. There was no legal action. Everyone knew that it was an accident, but Uncle Louie felt very bad about that incident.

The team continued their tour of the country. They played game after game in front of tens of thousands of Japanese fans. The players gathered in the clubhouse after each game to collect their pay, which they would immediately spend on whiskey and women. The players waited in the clubhouse after the final game on the exhibition schedule, but the promoter never showed. They found out that not only had this guy been skimming off the top but also this time he had taken the entire proceeds from the gate and skipped the country. The players, who had been living high on the hog from game to game, suddenly found themselves broke and abandoned in Japan. They sought help from the United States Consulate who arranged for their transport back to the states.

Uncle Louie was as famous back home for being a ladies' man as he was for being an athlete. My dad told me that at the onset of World War II he had given

Louie a bad time about possibly shooting at some of his kids when he fought the Japs. The sad thing about Uncle Louie was that he was good enough to have played pro ball, but it wasn't to be. He surrendered to the negative spirits of whiskey.

After the war, Uncle Louie participated in the annual entourage of brothers, uncles, and cousins of the George clan as they traveled in a large caravan across the mountains to hunt mule deer in eastern Washington. At that time, it was still permissible for Indians to hunt on their Tribal Identity Card, a promise made to us by treaty. The George clan took up a lot of space under the stars . . . twenty to thirty vehicles were parked between the trees. A large, moldy, canvas army tent was home away from home. It had a wood stove in one corner and sheets of plywood that covered the muddy floor. Everyone had a cot to sleep on except Uncle Louie. Grandpa said Uncle Louie wouldn't be caught dead sleeping in a tent. He would dress in his wool clothes and his pea coat, pull his watch cap down over his head, and sit in a pile of moss at the base of a tree some distance from camp with a bottle in his pocket and his gun across his lap, and there he would spend the night.

A Washington State Game Warden drove into camp one night. The George clan was sitting around the fire drinking whiskey and spinning tales. The warden insisted on checking everyone's Indian Card. Checking cards was well within his right, but this guy did it in a way that suggested a certain degree of disrespect. The guy was being a real jerk. Some of the George brothers took exception and started mouthing off.

Uncle Cees approached the warden, pulled him aside, and proceeded to tell him where the bear shit in the woods. "Listen, officer," he said, "we got a guy named Louie who likes to sleep out there in the trees. He's out there right now, sleepin'. If he wakes up and sees you here, there's no telling what he might do. Sometimes he gets to drinkin' and then he gets all worked up and excited. Wouldn't surprise me if he up and squeezes off a couple of rounds in your general direction. We just never know what Louie's gonna do next. You might just wanna get the hell outta here while the gittin' is good."

The warden was pissed. "Are you threatening me?"

Uncle Cees just smiled. "No, sir, just trying to tell you the way it is." The guy left in a huff, promising that he'd be back.

The next day, the warden showed up again. This time he had the County Sheriff in tow. The sheriff checked everyone's Indian Card, and on the way out of camp suggested, in no uncertain terms, that threatening a Washington State Game Officer would not be looked upon as acceptable behavior. Late that night the warden came back again, saying he wanted to talk to this Uncle Louie guy in person. He said he didn't believe the story about some drunken Indian that slept out in the sticks by himself. Uncle Cees pointed off into the distant woods where Louie's cigarette glowed in the darkness. "There he is. You go ahead on out there and have your talk. I wish you good luck. Try to make plenty of noise just in case."

The Game Warden apparently had second thoughts about talking with Uncle Louie. He hopped back in his truck and drove away. He visited the camp several more times . . . but only when the sun was high in the sky.

On those Eastern Washington trips, Uncle Benny was probably the best hunter in camp. Year after year Benny got his deer. Benny never hunted for sport. He hunted for subsistence. Uncle Benny was quite fond of wild coots, and when I was a boy, he would give me one box of shotgun shells for every three coots I brought by his house. Coots are sea birds that sit on the surface and dive for fish. My friends and I would shoot them from shore. We didn't have a dog so we had to do our own retrieving. We would paddle out on a piece of plywood or plank . . . anything that floated. If there was nothing to use for a makeshift raft and the birds weren't washed ashore by the waves, we took turns swimming out and retrieving them. We would get four or five birds on a good day. Coot hunting kept me in shotgun shells for many years.

Uncle Benny was a cagey old coot himself. Sometimes he would unexpectedly drop by the house to tell me it was time to fill up some gunnysacks with clams. "Come on, son, it's time to trade clams for some elk," he would say. We would drive up to the Quinault Reservation and deliver clams to Grandma George's contact in the Quinault Tribe. In exchange, we would get explicit hunting directions. "Go down logging road 2620 until you hit 2610. Then, turn left and drive in six-tenths of a mile. At about ten o'clock tonight the elk will come through."

On this particular night the wind was blowing and it was rainy and cold . . . typical Northwest weather. We followed the directions to the secret spot. My aunt dropped us off and drove the station wagon around in a large circle on the back roads. Uncle Benny and I crawled through the brush until we found a good sitting spot in an alder bottom. Uncle Benny gave me the flashlight. His rifle was loaded with twenty-two hollow-point magnums.

The sun went down and the rain fell, and it was so dark that we couldn't see our hand in front of our face. Around ten o'clock that night we were surrounded by the sound of snapping twigs and rattling bushes. "Turn the light on, Emerson. Shine'em," Uncle Benny whispered. I flipped the switch on the flashlight, and to my great delight, and Uncle Benny's complete horror, we found ourselves smack dab in the middle of a huge elk herd, surrounded by dozens of pairs of eyes. I was ecstatic.

"Shoot one, Uncle, shoot one!" I whispered.

Uncle Benny reached over and turned the flashlight out. "Be very quiet and don't move!"

"What's wrong, Uncle?"

"This is not good," he said. "If I shoot one of these animals, the rest of them could stampede and trample us."

I was no longer anxious for the kill. We sat there in silence for what seemed like an eternity. I was afraid to even breathe. Uncle Benny, in a hushed voice, finally broke the tension. "Oh, what the hell," he said, "I can't stand it. Shine'em, son, shine'em."

I turned on the flashlight, and the beam lit up a big cow elk less than twelve feet away. Uncle Benny took aim and shot her right above the left eye. She dropped like a sack of potatoes. The rest of the herd jumped a little and then casually walked on by and kept on going like they didn't have a care in the world. We quartered the elk, hauled it up to the road, and loaded it into the back of the wagon.

Back at Grandma George's house in Suquamish, the entire extended George clan would show up to help butcher and divide up the meat. Uncle Ted was usually there and I remember seeking him out. He would always take the time to talk with me and answer my questions. From politics to racism to Indian rights, Uncle Ted had a special way of explaining the way things were . . . things that nobody else seemed to talk about.

Uncle Ted was the only one of my aunts and uncles to complete a college education. He was appointed by President Nixon to sit in a prestigious position for Indian education. He was very intelligent and had a degree in Education. He taught school in several Washington cities, including Sumner and Yakima. Uncle Ted was in line to be the Director of the National Administration of Native Americans, a very prestigious position in an organization chartered to award grants and contracts in support of Indian programs. He was intensely analytical and had a special knack for putting things in the proper perspective. Uncle Ted was very influential in Indian country . . . soft spoken. He was a man who talked last and had the most to say.

When the treaties were signed with the Indians in the mid–1800s, the United States Government made several promises. They pledged to set aside reservation land for the natives. They guaranteed educational and health benefits, and they promised to pay the Indians for the land they were forced to give up, or cede.

Congress ratified the Indian treaties. However, the money to pay the Indians for their ceded land never made it into the hands of the Indians. That money is still there, and the government more or less concedes that they still owe that debt. The money for providing educational and health benefits was never appropriated. The only thing that the government actually did in accordance with the treaty was to take the land and move the Indians onto the reservations.

This issue of not paying the Indians for their ceded land is to this day in constant turmoil. U.S. Government officials and Indian leaders are trying to resolve the issue almost daily. I personally have serious doubts that there will be a resolution in my lifetime. I believe that the United States Government has an obligation under treaty to make things right. I'm not sure that the United States Treasury prints enough money to buy Indian tribes out.

Uncle Ted was a participant in a high-level meeting between government attorneys and national Indian leaders seeking to resolve the issue of compensation for ceded land. After days of fruitless negotiations, the government attorneys tendered what they claimed was their final offer. "The United States Government," they proposed, "offers to pay the Indian tribes of this country the sum of ten cents an acre for all ceded lands."

The Indian representatives at the meeting were outraged. Ten cents an acre was the going price 150 years ago. Verbal exchanges between the Indian leaders and the government officials were heated. Uncle Ted had listened in silence for several days as everyone spoke. Finally, he stood and cleared his throat. The room fell silent. "Gentlemen," he said, eyes scanning the room, "the Indian tribes have heard your gracious proposal and we are prepared to make a counter offer." The government officials leaned forward in their chairs. "We offer to buy back the ceded land for ten cents an acre." The government attorneys packed their briefcases and left the room in a huff. The meeting was over.

11 | With the Makah

I SPENT MY FIRST SIX YEARS AMONG THE MAKAH INDIANS ON THE Northwest tip of Washington state. My dad found work as a boilermaker at the Air Force radar site that sat high on the hills above the Makah Indian Reservation. The town of Neah Bay on the reservation existed primarily on the income from fishing, and the waters of the Strait of Juan De Fuca were rich with salmon and bottom fish. People came from around the world to fish for giant halibut and trophy-size king salmon.

I used to watch the flashlights and lanterns down on the fishing dock in the early morning. They looked like fireflies. The dock had a unique smell, and during fishing season the place was always busy . . . coolers being filled with ice, fresh herring being scooped and bagged, and scores of fishermen everywhere, loading poles and tackle boxes into their boats for a day's outing.

My dad would often take my brother and me down to the docks after the early morning rush, and while Dad passed a bottle with his friends, we would sit and watch the stragglers and latecomers launch their boats and motor past the breakwater, disappearing into the fog. When the bite was off, the dock was very quiet until late afternoon when a steady stream of cold and tired fishermen would motor in, tie up their boats, and trudge up the pier. If the fishing was good, there was a rush of activity. I loved to hang around the fish-cleaning stations and watch the seagulls fight over the entrails. My dad and my uncles would clean their morning catch and save the egg sacs from the hens. The salmon roe was a tasty treat, though Dad usually cured most of it for steelhead fishing.

I earned my sea legs on the deck of my father's 24-foot boat, the *Curtis C.*

Sometimes the rough water and the smell of the gas fumes from the open engine would make me seasick. One time I was feeling a bit queasy so I ate about a dozen mints—those round, red-orange mints about a quarter-inch thick—thinking it might settle my stomach. A very bad idea . . . the ultimate aversion therapy. To this day I can't stand to even look at those things.

My grandpa owned the 26' inboard, gray-hulled boat, the Twin. He often took me with him when he cruised up to Neah Bay from Suquamish. My grandpa and I would fill several gunnysacks full of little-neck steamers and manila clams from the beach in Suquamish. We would also dig butter clams, but because they spoiled quickly, we would shuck them and freeze them in mason jars. Grandpa taught me those types of clams could not be found on the beaches of Neah Bay, so they were as good as gold for trading favors with the Makah.

I used to stand on the back of the Twin and watch the boats disappear and re-appear with the ocean swells. I was only four or five years old at the time but somehow I reasoned that when the Twin was on top of the swell I could only see half of the boats. I will never forget the remarkable beauty of the place. The ocean waves crashed like thunder on the rocky shores. There were jagged pillars of rock that jutted out of the water. Sea birds circled and dove at schools of herring that liter-ally boiled on the surface. Sea lions and seals covered the rock outcroppings. I re-member laughing at the barking sound the sea lions made when my grandpa would steer the Twin too close. You could see eagles perched high on the cliffs in the skeletons of ancient trees, and it wasn't unusual to see pods of whales perform-ing a synchronized dance.

My grandfather pointed out special places along the shoreline. He had a story and a name for every point of land, every tree, and every cave that cut into the side of the cliffs. He told me many tales about the fish he had caught by the mushroom-shaped rock and how the large Chinook salmon would migrate along the line of thick kelp that hugged the shore. "Emerson," he would say, sadly shaking his head, "you should have seen this place when I was a boy. You should have seen it then." I never understood what he meant. I couldn't imagine it ever being more beauti-ful. I understand now. I have seen drastic changes in my short lifetime.

Many times the fog would slip in from the ocean and capture the boats in a thick, wet blanket. Somehow Dad and Grandpa would find their way back to the breakwater. One time a strong gale blew in from the west and whipped the water into a choppy, white froth. I was scared to death, clinging on to the railing. The wind was howling, and huge waves were breaking over the bow of the boat. I looked up at my dad's face for reassurance, and he was laughing and whooping it up like a rodeo rider on a wild bronco. I wasn't afraid after that.

My dad and grandpa had a special place they would go when they were out in the ocean and the weather turned nasty. They would pilot the Curtis C and Twin into a small, protected harbor that they called Ole's Hole. They would put the boats at anchor, and we would climb the rock bank to a cave that cut deep into the cliff. It was dry in there and sheltered from the wind. My dad would start a driftwood fire where I could warm my cold hands and feet. I have very special memories of Ole's Hole. It was a sanctuary.

I went back to Ole's Hole as a young man. I was curious and I wanted to study the place from a new perspective. I planned on descending to Ole's Hole from the landside, but as I stood high atop the near vertical cliffs and gazed down at the powerful surf crashing against the razor-sharp, jagged rocks, it came to me that maybe childhood memories are best left as childhood memories.

Fishing lasted throughout the summer. We smoked or dried most of the salmon that we caught for later use. There was never a shortage of whiskey aboard the Twin or the Curtis C, and when a salmon took the bait, my dad would toss an empty whiskey bottle into the water. The bottle would stay with the fish and the boat would stay with the bottle, and we would fill our coolers with salmon.

When fishing was slow, there was always something to do on the Makah Reservation. One of my favorite places was a small creek that trickled down from the hills and flowed through the field behind our house. I spent many days wading in that creek. I often stood still in the ankle-deep water, my hands on my knees, and watched hundreds of salmon smolt make their way downstream.

There was an old Makah woman that everyone called Grandma Allibush. All of us kids learned many secrets from her. In the spring she would take us along as she gathered bundles of salmonberry and red thimbleberry sprouts. She would take the sprouts home and put them up, and there were always enough fresh sprouts left over as a treat for us kids. I was quite fond of salmonberry sprouts . . . very tender morsels.

Grandma Allibush took special care to teach us the uses for a variety of plants, roots and berries that grew wild on the reservation. She was fond of the blackberries that grew on the other side of her fence, and she taught us that they were excellent to eat. One day I was standing on an old apple crate picking blackberries, and I slipped and fell. I landed on the fence, and a large wooden sliver from the side of the picket broke off and stuck in my neck. My mom fished it out with a pair of tweezers and painted the wound with iodine. I remember it was very painful, but I didn't cry out—not wanting to disappoint my dad.

One time, Dad took my cousin and me to the Makah Days' Celebration in town. The street was lined with booths and tables that were filled with food and trinkets. Hundreds of people were laughing and having fun. The wonderful smell of fresh popcorn filled the air, and for a nickel you could buy a sticky, web-like ball of cotton candy.

I remember the time my dad pulled us over to the dock where a large crowd had gathered in a circle. I broke free and crawled my way to the center of the circle where I found Bing Crosby and Phil Harris laughing and signing autographs. They had come to the reservation to fish and participate in the festivities. I must have been quite the sight with my little head sticking out between a forest of legs. Bing Crosby looked down, winked, and smiled at me. That vision is still very strong in my mind.

We didn't have a lot of money but that didn't stop Dad from taking Greg and me to the Airbase Theater to see *Abbott and Costello Meet the Mummy*. I had nightmares for days.

On Sundays all of us kids would run down to the jailhouse. We would hide in the bushes and watch as wives and relatives of the prisoners stood on stumps and chairs and exchanged laundry by passing the bundles through the bars on the windows . . . dirty clothes out, clean clothes in. Looking back on those days, I find it peculiar that my parents would allow us to watch the men behind bars but would make us come inside when the wild horses came down from the hills to romp and roll in the dusty field behind our house.

One afternoon several men knocked at the door. Dad followed them outside where they stood in a tight circle in the yard, passing a bottle of whiskey. They were talking very low and shaking their heads. I have a very vivid memory of Dad coming back into the house and telling my mom that some young man from the airbase had just jumped from the downtown bridge, breaking his neck. I remember looking up at my dad and asking him why that man would jump from the bridge and kill himself. "It is a way to escape, boy," he said, as he walked out the door, whiskey bottle in hand. "It is a way to escape." It was several days before Dad came home.

Dad never worked steady and we couldn't afford a television, so on Saturdays, when the *Lone Ranger* came on the radio, I would grab my six-shooter and Greg and I would sit cross-legged on the floor and listen to an exciting new adventure. In my mind's eye, I could see the Lone Ranger and Tonto riding the breakwater in pursuit of the bad guys. I would pretend I was the masked man. My six-shooter loaded with silver bullets was always strapped to my leg, ready for action. One year Grandpa Deam visited, and he brought me a holster and a white cowboy hat.

Grandpa Deam owned a retail fish store in Pine Bluff, Arkansas. He was a commercial fisherman, and he stocked his store with fish he himself had caught. Grandpa Deam was a rugged outdoorsman. He was a guide on the Arkansas River and part owner of hunting camps in Louisiana and Arkansas. He made a lot of money taking folks out hunting and fishing. Grandpa Deam showed up at Neah Bay once with his two bear hounds. He had won a bid to rid the Makah Reservation of fifty to seventy-five black bears that had become pests by rummaging around in the downtown garbage. I have an old photograph of Grandpa Deam and me in the back of his pickup truck. Grandpa Deam is holding a bear's head up by the ears, and I'm standing between Grandpa's legs smiling from ear to ear. Grandpa Deam kept his two bear hounds chained up alongside the house, and the area was soon dug up and covered with hair and dog poop. Grandpa Deam used to take me with him, and we'd feed his dogs yellow cornmeal mush from a metal bucket. I can still smell the foul stench.

I only saw Grandpa Deam a few times, but every year we would travel down to Suquamish to visit Grandma and Grandpa George. My mom always got carsick on the winding coast road between Neah Bay and Port Angeles. Dad would stop at the little store a couple of miles from Grandma George's house, and Greg and I would each get an ice cream drumstick for being good on the trip. We would both get ice cream headaches because Dad would tell us that we had to finish the ice cream before we got to Grandma's so the other kids wouldn't complain about being without.

Every year the entire extended family would travel up from Suquamish, gunnysacks of clams in hand, to fish for subsistence. An instant tent city would rise from the sand. I can still smell the musty scent of the green canvas. There was a special family closeness at these gatherings. Everyone pitched in to help. The men tied their sharp hooks and leaders; the women gathered roots and berries for the evening meal. The kids had the job of gathering driftwood to fuel the fire . . . and what a fire it was. When the sun went down and there was a bite to the air, the men would set a match to what my grandpa called the "bullshit fire." Everyone found a place in the sand to sit, and the spinning of excellent family stories would commence. The kids had the privilege of fueling the fire, and as Grandpa was fond of saying, "The bigger the fire, the bigger the bullshit." As the evening progressed, there was a lot of camaraderie and merriment between brothers, sisters, and cousins. The fire would get very large and very hot, and the stories would keep pace well into the night, fueled by an endless supply of beer and whiskey.

Every morning the men would be up early to fish, and every afternoon there were great drunken parties and salmon bakes on the beach. I looked forward to the succulent sand bread that my grandmother baked. She would build a large fire on the beach, push the fire off, and cover the dough with the hot sand. When the bread was done, she would pull it out and brush it off. The loaf was warm and golden brown, and there were seldom second helpings.

When I turned six, my parents—not too impressed with the quality of the schools on the Makah Reservation—moved the family back to Suquamish. I have walked down many paths since those early days at Neah Bay, but my awareness and my perception of who I am will always be filtered through the eyes of a boy who spent his youth with the Makah.

12 | On the Beach

I REMEMBER ONE SATURDAY MORNING IN THE EARLY FALL. I WAS upstairs in bed and my grandma called for me to come down to breakfast. I lay very still and closed my eyes, not to sleep but to listen. I could hear the crows fussing, the songbirds chirping, and the sound of the pebbles tumbling with the rhythm of the waves. I knew I had all day to go to the beach and fish and hunt for treasures. I dressed in my jeans and my wool fishing shirt. I could smell Grandma's fresh coffee and warm biscuits. Grandma George always made a good breakfast with thick bacon, large brown eggs, and fresh bread that she would bake in the cast iron oven the night before. I went into the bathroom and looked in the mirror. I could see my father in my face and it worried me. A splash of cold well water took the sleep from my eyes, and I hurried downstairs to my place at the table. Grandma touched my shoulder, as she always did, and placed my breakfast in front of me. "Good morning, young man," she would say. "Three eggs or four?" It was a game Grandma and I had played since I was a small boy. "I can eat all that you have, Grandma, but this morning I will just have two."

Grandpa was standing in the corner of the room. He was very quiet. His body was rigid and his eyes were riveted to the counter top as if he were deep in thought. I had only seen him so transfixed and focused when we sat together in the bushes stalking game.

"Grandpa, are you all right?"

Grandpa George always spoke very slowly and deliberately. "Yes," he said, "I am fine. It is this toaster. It is smarter than me. It somehow knows when the toast is done." I laughed at his funny joke.

Grandpa said nothing. He walked to the table and sat in his favorite chair. He picked up the percolator and filled his mug with hot coffee. I could see no humor in his eyes, and I knew it was best to say nothing. I was working on a spreadsheet the other night on my computer, and I remembered that story as the spreadsheet instantly performed page after page of complex calculations, and I knew what my grandpa had meant because that computer was definitely smarter than I was.

I grabbed several of Grandma's warm biscuits from the pan on the table and crammed them into the pocket of my jacket. I rushed out the door and grabbed my fishing pole and tackle box from the back porch. The tide was low and there were many things to do. I ran down the narrow path that led to the water. A small squirrel chattered to me as it scurried across an old rotting cedar tree and up to its home in the branches above. I stopped at the edge of the beach where large, smooth pebbles had been piled in gentle ridges by the waves. I closed my eyes and breathed in the wonderful smell of seaweed and exposed barnacles. It was a fragrance I would always know.

There was an old wooden boat that had been lying up against a large chunk of driftwood for as long as I could remember. I thought about patching her up once so I could use her as a fishing skiff, but the wood had dry rot in places and there was a gaping hole in the bow. Greg and I sat in the boat many times pretending we were warriors doing battle with an endless stream of imaginary enemies.

On a minus tide the newly exposed beach was mostly gray sand and large boulders. If you turned over the rocks, you could sometimes expose a bullhead or an eel, and there would always be an explosion of small crabs rushing for cover in all directions. The tiny crabs made excellent bait. I had an old metal bucket that I kept hidden under some driftwood next to the boat, and I would put a dozen or so scurrying crabs into the bucket for later use. Sometimes there were hundreds of birds that dove and fussed about out on the surface of the water. Grandpa George taught me that the birds were feeding on large herring balls.

All along the water's edge you could see the extended necks of horse clams and geoducks (goo-ee-duck). Geoducks are giant clams. Their long, thick necks protrude from the sand and are visible during extremely low tides. They are also found in abundance below the tide line in the deeper waters of Puget Sound. When you got too close, they would squirt and retreat into the sand. I didn't have a shovel, but the cupped edge of a large geoduck shell worked great for dredging a hole in the sand. The sides of the hole would collapse as I dug, and water would constantly seep in and fill the hole. I could scoop up handful after handful of water and sand, and it wouldn't take me long to fill the bucket with clams.

When the tide turned, the incoming water would quickly cover the clam beds, and I would haul the bucket up on the beach and clear a spot in the sand for a driftwood fire. I would fill the bucket with seawater and boil the clams until the shells opened. I would then sit by the fire, the salt breeze blowing through my hair, and feast on the succulent morsels.

When the tide was high, we would fish for whatever there was to catch: cod, perch, flounder, it didn't matter. We would catch bullheads and brand them. We all had our own brand. Mine was two slashes away from the head. We would see how many times the same bullhead could be caught. We used to fish for birds. We would take a glob of hamburger or a glob of bacon or a hotdog and put it up on the rail of the pier. Then we'd let out the line, walk up onto the shore and sit and wait. The gulls and crows would always come.

The days always seemed to pass quickly on the beach, and when the sun was low in the sky, it was time to head back. We would stash the bucket in its hiding place and pour a bucket of seawater on our fire, using a stick to spread the coals. As we headed up the path to our grandparents' house, I remember always feeling uneasy knowing it was time to deal with going home.

13 | Dear Old Golden Rule Days

THE SUQUAMISH ELEMENTARY SCHOOL WAS SMALL WITH ONLY FOUR classrooms. The first grade class was in one room and the second through sixth grade classes doubled up in the other three rooms. There were very few Indian children enrolled. I was the only Indian in my class. There was a brother and sister a grade above me—and fewer than ten Indian children in the entire school.

I was enrolled in Mrs. Tallman's first grade class with ten others who would remain my friends and schoolmates through the grade school. Our morning-muster read like a B-movie theater marquee: Now showing, from the town of Suquamish, Randy Blossom, Barbara Lewis, B. J. Castleberry, Ruth Tarbull and Rollin Doe. Rollin was my neighbor and was also in my Scout troop. Befitting his name, Rollin Doe would grow up to be a used car salesman.

I sat at a wooden desk in the back of the room. The desk had seen better days. Several previous students had gouged their initials in the top for posterity, and someone had carved the letter *A* in the lower-right-hand corner. I learned where I could put my paper so that my pencil wouldn't break through when I practiced my letters.

Every Friday after school the janitor would spread fresh oil on the hardwood floors. The oil was thick, and the excess residue would build up in the crevices and around the edges. On Monday mornings the school smelled like oil. I loved that smell. When we came back to school each week and gathered in the hallway to hang up our coats, if it was raining the rainwater would drip from our lunch pails and raingear and pool up in tiny beads on the floor, glistening like so many diamonds.

I was never accused of glistening as a student. I had a rough time with school. My reading and penmanship skills were very poor. Like many Indian kids, I seldom got around to doing my homework, and I found it very difficult to concentrate on my lessons. The problems that complicated my formal education are still very prevalent on the reservation today. Teachers hammer Indian children for their failure to turn in homework assignments, when many of them walk home from school to the burden of an alcoholic environment, many of them unsure of where they will sleep that night or even when they can expect their next meal. Being studious is a luxury that many Indian children can ill afford.

My favorite subject in grade school was recess. I spent a lot of time staring up at the clock waiting for the bell. I used to daydream . . . imagining myself in some faraway land where there were treasures to discover, dragons to slay, and battles to win. While my teacher was expounding on the historical significance of dumping a shipload of tea into the bay to protest of taxation without representation, I was hiding in the bushes on the banks of the White River preparing to do battle alongside Sealth. The teacher calling out my name would bring me back, but apparently only after repeating "Emerson" four or five times to the giggling amusement of my classmates.

One morning I had to pee so badly I couldn't stop squirming in my chair, and the clock was two minutes away from the recess bell. The bathroom at the school was downstairs, and I was so worried about wasting precious recess time that I unzipped my fly in the classroom so that I could take a leak the second I got to the boys' room. When the bell rang I was off like a shot. As I rounded the corner going down the up staircase, some young girl coming up the stairs yelled out to me that my pants were unzipped. I yelled back without missing a step, telling her that I was in a hurry.

I was first to the bathroom but was soon joined by several other boys, including Rollin Doe and Delbert Norberg. Delbert was somewhat of a school celebrity. It was widely rumored that Delbert Norberg possessed a certain special talent that had to be seen to be believed, and I was fortunate enough to bare witness that day to one of his marquee performances. Delbert positioned himself on top of the end of the long urinal in an unprecedented display of balance and physical prowess. He had unzipped his fly, and to the oohs and ahs of his gathered audience, he pissed all the way over the top of the wall. We let out a collective sigh of admiration. Nobody else could do that but Delbert Norberg . . . it was so cool. Rollin and I were very impressed. I'm not sure Rollin ever did go to the bathroom that day. Maybe he figured he'd pale by comparison.

After school, when it was time to head homeward, I would stop by the church and just sit in a pew and think, or I would wander down to the beach and skip rocks, anything to delay going home. Even school seemed more of a sanctuary than a place to learn things, though there was one special teacher, a Mrs. Garrett, who had a profound impact on my life.

Mrs. Garrett taught third grade at Suquamish Elementary. She lived on Bainbridge Island, and I think she had a degree in history from Gonzaga University. Mrs. Garrett had a special kinship for Native folks. She understood that a healthy cultural identity would be the only hope many of her Indian students would have to avoid the cycle of poverty and alcoholism that has plagued my people for generations. I had the great fortune of being in her class.

Around Thanksgiving, Mrs. Garrett selected me and two other Indian students to help her build a model of a historical Suquamish Indian village. She helped us sprinkle white sand and tiny shells on the edge of a mirror that simulated the Puget Sound. Together we built a small wooden replica of the Old Man Longhouse, and we made cutout teepees from white craft paper. I had a store-bought canoe at home that I played with in the bathtub. I brought it to school and placed it on the mirror.

Mrs. Garrett took great pains to involve the entire class in the project. She told us about the Longhouse that Sealth's father had built on the beach in Suquamish and how Sealth had fought a great battle on the White River and was chosen as Chief of the United Tribes for his bravery and wisdom.

That project had a powerful impact on me. I realized for the first time what it meant to be a Suquamish Indian, and for the first time I felt great pride in my heritage. Mrs. Garrett gave the three of us a sense of ourselves that year. For me, the realization of my cultural identity was the key to all of my future accomplishments and would send me down a lifelong path of self-discovery.

14 | Squarehead and Dumb Dumb

MY FAMILY LIVED IN A SMALL, ONE-BEDROOM HOUSE UP ON THE hill, very close to the school, and two doors down from the Congregational Church. Greg and I didn't have our own bedroom. We slept in the living room on a couch that folded out into a bed. Our house was always warm and cozy. Dad heated with wood, and once the fire was lit it would burn all winter. In the evening, before the family went to bed, Dad would stick in a chunk of the three-inch thick, old-growth bark and damper the wood stove down. The bark would smolder all night and leave hot embers for igniting the next day's fire. Dad was fond of burning fir. I hated fir. Fir wood was full of slivers, and I could find no way to avoid being painfully impaled.

My grandpa, my dad, and my uncles got together every summer to cut up windfalls. One uncle would limb, one would buck, and my dad would split . . . cold beer and whiskey would always be prevalent. Grandpa George had one of those old drag saws, the ones with a one-cylinder piston engine. The saw had a six-foot, single, crosscut blade and would cut on the forward stroke and ride a guide on the backstroke. Grandpa used to lean that drag saw against an old-growth downfall and fire it up. The drag saw would cut through the log in about fifteen minutes. You could hear the steady chug, chug, chug of the engine echoing through the forest. Greg and I always got stuck with packing and stacking cord after cord for each family. All of our cousins would always mysteriously disappear.

On the weekends and during the summer, there were plenty of neighborhood kids to play with, including my first cousin, Chuck Deam. My mom and Chuck's dad were brother and sister. I also spent a lot of my free time playing with Nelson Theodore. Everyone referred to Nelson as Dumb Dumb. Nelson was an Indian kid born with fetal alcohol syndrome, though at the time nobody knew there was such a thing. Nelson's parents just figured that he was stupid or retarded and they nicknamed him Dumb Dumb. The name stuck and Nelson, at least on the surface, seemed to accept the label with indifference.

Nelson lived right next door to us, and we used to pick blackberries and salmonberry sprouts together. I always felt comfortable hanging out with Dumb Dumb. I was a runt, and he wasn't too bright, and we just made a good team. I guess I never felt the need to compete with him, and I suppose that made for a special bond.

Nelson's grandparents, Joe and Lena Hilliar, were both widowed when they met. Each of them brought several children into that marriage, so there were always plenty of people in their house. The Hilliar place was stereotypically Indian, from the smelly drain field and a collection of old rusted cars to the broken washer and dryer in the backyard. In the summertime cascara bark covered the roof of their house. Cascara bark was a cash crop. Joe would fell a cascara tree and cut it into one-foot lengths. Then, he'd strip away the bark and get Nelson to lay it out on the roof to dry. Joe sold the dried cascara bark for use as a laxative.

Many Indian families had ways to make extra money—digging clams, catching salmon, cutting wood or picking brush. My dad picked a lot of brush, and Greg and I often went with him to help. The best salal and blueberry brush was found in forested areas with a high canopy. My dad knew all of the best picking spots. We sold the brush by the hand to the holly farm in Silverdale, and they used the brush for floral arrangements. A hand of brush was literally that, one handful. A good picker could pick forty or fifty hands a day and get anywhere from a buck or two per hand, depending on quality and demand.

Whenever Joe Hilliar went out to pick brush, he would stop by the tavern on the way home and drink up some of his earnings. A lot of times, late at night, I would lie awake in bed and listen to the drunken brawls and the screaming and hollering that came from the Hilliar house.

Fighting wasn't the only noise that came from the other side of the tall wooden fence that separated our back yards. Sometimes, in the early morning and after dinner, I would hear a steady chip, chip, chip. Joe Hilliar was a wood carver and a master craftsman. He was a Lummi Indian who had married Suquamish. Joe was about seventy years old, and his hair was long and braided. He used all of the traditional carving tools, including a variety of hand-made adzes and chisels. Some were made from iron, but many of his tools were made from stone. Joe even had some special draw tools that he had made using leaf springs from an old car.

I often climbed up on the fence and watched him chip away at a log . . . chopping a little here, scraping a little there. I asked him once why he didn't take bigger cuts, and he told me that when it came to carving wood that twelve little cuts were much better than one big cut. I didn't understand what he meant until, after watching him slowly chip away at that log for weeks, I could see a wondrous face and form appear from the heart of the wood. The skill and precision of his strokes fascinated me. One day he broke the handle on an adz, and I watched him use strips of yew wood to lash the metal to a new handle. Joe was always yelling at Nelson to get out from under his feet while he worked. Dumb Dumb really liked his grandpa and loved to watch him carve, but Nelson always seemed to be doing the wrong things at the wrong time. Joe would eventually lose his patience, along with his temper, and Dumb Dumb would end up on the other side of the fence next to me. We must have spent hundreds of hours watching Joe work. I had no idea that I was watching history in the making from my own private, front-row seat.

As it turned out, Joe Hilliar was carving the totem pole that was erected at the 1962 Seattle World's Fair. I was thrilled to death when I found out, not only because I had witnessed its creation but also because the pole was, coincidentally, dedicated on my thirteenth birthday and represented the story of two boys seeking a vision through the sun in the sky. I remember watching Joe's face as important dignitaries made fancy speeches and offered him their hand in congratulations. I thought how proud Joe must be for what he had accomplished; yet there was sadness in his eyes. Later on, when my Grandpa and I were digging clams, I asked him why Joe had seemed so sad on a day when so many people were honoring his work.

Grandpa knelt down, grabbed a handful of dry sand, and let it sift through his fingers until it was gone. "Like the sand," he said, "Joe has finished his totem. Maybe Joe was sad because he knew that his work was finished. Remember, boy, the real joy in life is not found in the destination. It is found in the journey."

Joe's totem pole was eventually displayed throughout the United States and was even sent to Kobe, Japan, Seattle's sister city. Today, I can close my eyes and still see every detail of that totem pole. Sometimes, when I am awake in bed late at night, I can even hear the rhythmic sound of Joe chipping on his log.

At night, when the streets of your cities and villages
shall be silent and you think them deserted,
they will throng with the returning hosts
that once filled and still love this beautiful land.

The pole had a natural wood when it was carved. Today the pole has color, which was added later by one of Joe's grandsons using all natural dyes.

On the other side of the street from the Hilliar house lived one Sonny Olson. Sonny was the biggest, meanest, orneriest, White kid on the face of the earth. We all called him Squarehead, behind his back of course, and the name stuck. Squarehead was younger than both Dumb Dumb and me. He was built like a large bear, and like most bullies, he reigned over the neighborhood by waging a constant war of terrorism and intimidation. Squarehead took advantage of every available opportunity to pick on Dumb Dumb or subject me to numerous humbling indignities. He was fond of stealing my bicycle and taking it up to his house. I would have to stealthily sneak over under cover of darkness to snatch it back.

Though Squarehead was my archenemy, I was good friends with his older brother Danny. Danny was good people. He was a hippie in the '60s. His hair was bright red, and he sported an Afro hairdo that was a foot and a half in diameter. Whenever we called out to him, Danny would turn around and his hair would undulate from side to side like a big red Slinky. Old Man Squarehead wore a flat top with sideboards and had an attitude to match, so he and Danny never did quite see eye to eye. They just plain hated each other. The last time I saw Danny he was wearing leg-high buckskins with a Bowie knife strapped to his waist.

It wasn't hard to figure out why Danny hated his old man or why Sonny Squarehead was so ornery. Old Man Squarehead was always whaling on both of them for no particular reason. The Squarehead family owned a turd business, a septic service. When we were in high school, Old Man Squarehead worked swing shift. He used to make Sonny operate the turd truck. Sonny didn't get paid, probably because he wasn't much for following directions or paying attention to detail. One day we watched Sonny drive the truck into town with a length of three-inch hose still hooked onto the back, whipping across traffic. By the time he got home the hose was trashed. You would think that Squarehead had killed somebody the way his old man laid into him with a belt.

I had a healthy fear of Sonny Squarehead. Everyone did, but I always stood my ground. It pissed me off whenever Squarehead taunted Dumb Dumb and mocked him for his shortcomings. Dumb Dumb never seemed to mind, but I would be furious. I would yell at Squarehead and tell him to back off, but Sonny would only laugh and flick me in the head with his finger.

Our abuse at the hands of Squarehead eventually manifested itself into a deep-seated desire for justice and revenge, but I knew I couldn't compete with Squarehead's superior strength and size. I can't count how many times I came home with a cut lip or a bloody nose from a one-sided confrontation. My dad used to say, "Kid, if you can't kick their ass, then get yourself an equalizer."

My dad had a heavy old 36" wooden baseball bat that the older kids used to propel rocks into the woods. One day Squarehead had pushed me to the limit. I was seventy-five pounds of angry Indian when I stormed into the house and grabbed that bat. Barely able to lift it, I dragged it behind me through the living room, and as I passed Dad, he asked me what I was planning to do with his bat. I opened the front door and stormed outside. "This is my equalizer, Dad!" I yelled, as the screen door slammed behind me. Squarehead was standing in the middle of the street. He had Dumb Dumb in a half-nelson, no pun intended, and was giving him a noogie, thumping him in the head with his knuckles. I could feel my blood boil as an uncontrollable anger welled up inside me. "Come here, Sonny Squarehead!" I screamed. "Come here and get what's coming to ya!"

Sonny turned Nelson loose and laughed as Dumb Dumb fell face first to the concrete, bouncing off Squarehead's knee on the way down. Sonny walked in a beeline straight for me. His eyebrows were furrowed, and the intent to cause death and mayhem were etched across his Neanderthal face. I hoisted that bat up over my shoulder and stood poised to strike. I wanted to whack Sonny upside the head, but part of me was afraid I would kill him. So, when he was within range, I swung that bat with all of my strength and smacked him right across the legs. He seemed stunned for a second, and then he started to laugh a big old belly laugh. Squarehead grabbed the bat away from me and tossed it aside. He threw me to the ground, pinned me down with his knees on my arms, and commenced to beat on my face, laughing the entire time.

Dumb Dumb jumped on Squarehead's back but Sonny kept swinging like he didn't even notice. It took Sonny's dad and my dad to pull Squarehead off me. I lost the tops of my two front teeth from that pummeling, but I think I gained some respect in exchange. It was the last time Squarehead and I would ever fight. To this day there are still people in Suquamish who refer to Sonny Olson as Squarehead. I call him Sonny.

One day Dumb Dumb, Squarehead, Greg, and I chased some cats up a tree. The cats stayed up there for hours, meowing endlessly and refusing to budge. We decided we would climb the tree and knock them down. Greg went up the tree first with a stick, and one of the cats, not particularly pleased by his presence, swiped at him with her razor-sharp claws. Greg, being very athletic, jumped back and descended hand over hand down the limbs like a monkey. Sonny, being the way he was, bragged that he would go up and knock those stupid cats down. So Squarehead climbed the tree with the stick in his mouth. When he reached the first cat, he pulled the stick from between his teeth and drew it back like a baseball bat. The cat was having none of it and took a swipe at Sonny's head. He jumped back, the stick flew through the air, and Squarehead fell twenty feet, landing with a dull thud in a heap at the base of the tree. His head struck an old alder log, and it sounded like someone had whacked it with a sledgehammer. Squarehead lay there moaning with his eyes crossed. He had the breath knocked out of him. Eventually he got up and reverted to form, but for a good ten minutes, Dumb Dumb, Greg, and I laughed out loud with little fear of retaliation. Dumb Dumb was laughing so hard he peed in his pants.

Another favorite pastime was playing Swiss Family Robinson in the two tree houses we had built from wood scraps in the trees behind the church. It was a great hiding place where we could share a warm, stolen beer or pass a cigarette around to solidify friendships. We would ride our bikes back to the tree houses where, armed with bags full of pinecones, we would wage protracted wars for hours until it was too dark to see.

On the way back home we would fire off rounds of pinecones from our bikes or engage in spirited rounds of fender tag. Fender tag involved smacking the rear wheel of a fleeing rider's bike with your front wheel. That would transfer the honor of being "IT" to the person you tagged, and he would proceed to chase the other two.

My dad bought my bike used and had painted it pale blue. It had had large, fat, tube tires. That bike wasn't much to look at, but when powered by an endless supply of youthful energy, it became my primary mode of transportation. Neighborhood status and pecking order were determined by how many playing cards we could stick in the spokes with wooden clothespins. At one point, childhood etiquette dictated that bicycle handlebars should be turned upside-down. Try as I might, I could only spin the handlebars backwards and was unmercifully subjected to the wrath of Squarehead, whose laughter could be heard for blocks. Fortunately, my cousin, Chuck, was the mechanic in the family. He showed me how to remove the handgrips, pull the handlebars out, reverse them, and put them in upside-down.

Squarehead grew up in spite of himself and still lives in the Suquamish area. He works in construction. I no longer fear him, and I now consider Sonny Olson a friend. Besides, I am no longer a runt, and I'm sure I can outrun the grownup Squarehead, who weighs in at around 400 pounds.

Joe passed over and Dumb Dumb was never the same. He slowly drifted away from us. He became quiet and withdrawn. His way of dealing with his life, and the hand he had been dealt, was to spend ten cents at the hardware store for a tube of airplane glue. Sometimes I would hear sobbing coming from the other side of the fence, and I would peek over and see Nelson sitting on a stump, rocking back and forth, staring at the pile of rotting wood chips, tears running down his face. We found Nelson dead one day . . . he had hanged himself in his back yard. He was fourteen.

15 | Rusty Hooks

THAT INDIANS HAVE A DIFFICULT TIME WITH ALCOHOL IS A WELL-known fact. Whether the cause is genetic, cultural, spiritual, or something in the water does little to change that truth. Alcohol use, if not abuse, is as high as ninety percent on the Point Madison Reservation. The Port Gamble S'Klallam Tribe recently did a survey on their reservation and found some form of substance abuse in 198 out of 205 households.

My father was an alcoholic. He was also a highly decorated veteran of World War II, and he used the horrors he had witnessed on the battlefield as justification for his affliction. He told me many times that drinking helped him to cope with his recurring nightmares of that horrible conflict. I listened to that explanation many times, but it could never explain why my aunts and uncles were all alcoholics. They didn't fight in the war.

My father was not a violent man. He was a happy drunk. He never struck my mom, and he never hit my brother and me . . . nor did he hug or encourage us. He would just disappear once in awhile. He had his regular stop on the way home from work at a place he called Shady Rest. Sometimes he would stay there for two or three hours, and sometimes he wouldn't come home until long after I was in bed. One time Dad confided in me that, by his best guess, he had consumed $30,000 worth of whiskey at Shady Rest. This was not social drinking with the good old boys at the corner bar over a game of pool. Shady Rest was an isolated side road on top of a hill on a piece of property owned by Grandma George. My dad was not only the bartender . . . he was the only customer.

There was a tavern about six blocks from our house, however. Mom would always pull me aside and tell me to go with Dad and keep him out of the bar. Greg and I would hop in the back seat of the car, and Dad would inevitably stop at the tavern for drinks. I had no chance of convincing him otherwise. I sat in the car and waited for hours knowing that I had let my mother down. Greg would just leave after awhile and walk home, but I was the oldest son and I felt a responsibility to stay in the car until Dad was done. There were several times I sat there for the entire evening. Dad would show us his conditional love by bringing us a soda from the bar or by giving each of us thirty-five cents for a Coke and candy bar at the grocery store. The standing rule was that we had to duck down in the back seat whenever a car drove by because if a cop saw us unattended outside of the tavern Dad would be arrested.

Mom was numb. She went to Alcoholics Anonymous meetings on a regular basis, but I believe her preferred method for coping was to just not deal with anything. She turned her emotions and her feelings inward. She surrounded herself with a hard shell, and there she would hide for safety, protected from everything and everyone, including Greg and me, who desperately needed her approval, love, and affection.

I suppose we suffered far less from abuse than we did from apathy, though I suppose one could argue the two are one and the same. There was no love or compassion. There was no understanding or communication. There was no support or encouragement. There was nothing but dysfunction. For me there were only two choices . . . imitation or escape. I chose escape.

I was a box boy at the IGA store in downtown Suquamish. I also had a paper route and worked both jobs simultaneously. I turned out for high school wrestling even though I was a runt. I weighed less that 100 pounds soaking wet. I wrestled ferociously but seldom won a match. I won the most inspirational award for my class, not for my wrestling prowess but because I tried so hard.

I found sanctuary in the neighborhood Congregational Church, and I would spend many an evening there. Scouting, like church, was an activity that offered a stable, sober environment unlike the dysfunction that awaited me at home. Scouting also offered acceptance for who I was and what I could do and helped me develop leadership skills. I learned about citizenship in the home, in the community, and in the nation. I developed a great deal of pride in the Suquamish community, and I participated in paper drives and many other community functions.

I worked my butt off to be eligible for Eagle Scout consideration by earning numerous mandatory and optional merit badges. Each merit badge signified a specific life skill that I studied, practiced, and mastered, and I seemed to excel at knot tying, canoeing, archery, marksmanship, and hiking—all types of activities that lend themselves to the outdoor way of life.

Attaining the rank of Eagle Scout is a great honor. It is the culmination of years of continued effort and hard work. For every one hundred boys who join the Scouts, only one makes Eagle Scout. The time came for me to stand before an Eagle Board of Review. The Board was comprised of community leaders, including then Mayor Glenn Jarstad of Bremerton as well as the Commander of Puget Sound Naval Shipyard. The event was broadcast on local television. The selected candidates answered pointed questions from the Board about our accomplishments and experiences.

Standing before the Review Board was one of the scariest moments of my life. I was looking good though. My uniform was pressed and my buttons were polished. When the Review Board awarded me the rank of Eagle Scout, I was probably the proudest Indian boy on the Port Madison Indian Reservation . . . the first Eagle Scout in the history of Suquamish!

Eagle Scouts are required to perform a community project. I convinced one of my teachers in junior high to open the school gym for two or three hours on Tuesday and Thursday nights. I organized basketball and soccer games. I borrowed bows and arrows from the Scout office and opened up archery classes. For two years, twice a week, that gym would vibrate with the happy voices of dozens of kids.

I was one of sixty young men selected from Washington state to attend the first World Boy Scout Jamboree to be held in the United States. The Jamboree, located in Farragut State Park four miles east of Athol, Idaho, would host 10,000 Scouts from around the world. I shared my campfire and my heritage with Scouts from many countries. I came to understand their differing customs, values and lifestyles. I met actor Jimmy Stewart at the Jamboree. I also met Wally Shirrah, one of the original Mercury astronauts, whose Mercury capsule was set up on display. Vice-President Hubert Humphrey was in attendance, as were the governors of Washington and Idaho. My group was chosen to participate in an open forum between Governor Dan Evans of Washington, the governor of Idaho, and important national tribal leaders.

American Legion Post 60 funded the trip to the World Jamboree, as well as numerous camping and hiking excursions. The Chief Seattle Days' Celebration, for example, was initially just a salmon bake put on by the Legion to raise money for these events. My dad would arrange to buy fish, and the American Legion would use the old Nike site at Kingston to shred cabbage and put together a meal. The totem pole, carved by Joe Hillier for the 1962 Seattle World's Fair, was erected in downtown Suquamish for the event. One of our Scoutmasters contacted the Order of the Arrow dance group from the Chief Seattle Council in Seattle. The group agreed to perform their showcase of traditional Indian dances, and over 10,000 people showed up for the event. The American Legion would make anywhere from $2,000 to $4,000, and that money would be used to provide Scouting opportunities for dozens of Suquamish children who couldn't otherwise afford to participate.

The Chief Seattle Days' Celebration was also an excellent forum for showcasing the fascinating history and rich culture of the Suquamish people. Tribal members prepared the salmon dinner and conducted guided tours of historical sites, including Chief Sealth's grave and the ruins of the Old Man House. The Tribal Center was decorated with tribal art and historical artifacts. Joe Hilliar's totem pole was always a popular attraction. The Chief Seattle Days' Celebration put the Port Madison Indian Reservation on the map.

The activity most favored by us kids in the neighborhood was the American Legion's Annual Kid's Fishing Derby. Every year my uncles would show up at the house for the event. Uncle Cees was my favorite uncle. He was very close to my dad. I remember that whenever Uncle Cees had too much to drink he would say he was "feeling too good." When Uncle Cees was feeling too good, he always managed to find his way to our house for something to eat.

The doors were never locked, so Uncle Cees would just walk in, have a snack, and leave. My mom used to stick little cupcake-shaped, baking soda cakes in the refrigerator to absorb odors. Uncle Cees paid one of his unscheduled visits two days before the fishing derby. I found teeth marks and a bite missing in one of those deodorizer cakes. Apparently, Uncle Cees was feeling way too good to notice that this particular pastry recipe was a bit too heavy on the baking soda.

The night before the fishing derby had finally arrived. My uncles had showed up on cue and Uncle Cees was, as always, feeling too good. Dinner was served, and the conversation around the table seldom strayed from the issue at hand . . . catching the winning fish. This fishing derby was a special time for Greg and me. It was one of the few family rituals that we were always able to count on. Dad would break out the whiskey and the beer and tie fishing leaders. He tied a special knot, and he always used the sharpest of hooks. Dad took great care in teaching us his secret hook-tying technique. He separated each tied hook by sticking them in a neat row on a piece of cardboard.

I had the tickets tucked away in my wallet. I had pulled them out often that week to gaze upon them and daydream about the big fish I would surely catch. I envisioned myself proudly riding that first-place bike through downtown Suquamish, playing cards in the spokes and head held high.

Dad was not there for dinner but it wasn't unusual for him to show up late. Greg and I cleared the plates while the adults retired to the living room. We sat at the kitchen table for over an hour and stared out the window. The time for tying hooks had come and gone and there was no sign of Dad. Greg got up and left the table without speaking. I sat at the kitchen table by myself. I had a lump in my throat. I stared out the window hoping to see the lights of the family truck weaving down the dirt driveway. Dad had never missed a fishing derby. I could hear my uncles in the other room getting louder and more boisterous with every tip of the bottle. The tears soon welled up in my eyes and ran down my cheeks.

I had learned at a young age that survival depended on the ability to compromise and improvise. I was not willing to sacrifice an opportunity to win that bike. Greg and I would fish in the derby one way or another. I reasoned that we could go out with our uncle and his son. I put on a brave face and called out to Greg,

"Come here," I yelled. "Let's get ready to go fishing."

We dug out Dad's tackle box and set it up on the kitchen table. Greg opened the latch and we stared inside. There was an old spool of fishing line . . . most of it was gone. There were several sinkers, rusty swivels, a broken knife, and two rusty spoons. I picked up the spoons and held them in the palm of my hand. I was very disheartened. I knew that the rusty spoons with their rusty hooks would catch nothing. "These will do," I said, trying to encourage Greg. "These spoons will win us that bike."

The next morning we were up early. The sun was an hour away. We dressed warmly and hurried down to the kitchen. Dad was slouched over the table, his head resting in his hands. I walked to the stove and warmed up that morning's coffee in the aluminum percolator. I poured what there was in a cup and placed it on the table in front of Dad. Greg and I sat down across from him, hands folded, and watched him sip from the cup. For the longest time nobody spoke . . . there was nothing to be said.

When Dad finished the coffee he held the empty cup in his hands and stared at the tabletop. He muttered something, but I didn't understand his words. Finally, he stood up, put on his coat, and headed for the door. "Let's catch fish," he said. Greg and I grabbed our gear and shot out the door, running down the dirt path ahead of Dad who was walking a bit funny and still showing the effects of a lengthy stay at Shady Rest. We launched the boat and fished for over an hour in silence. The salmon did not come to the bait.

Dad sat in the back of the boat, his right hand on the throttle. His eyes were half closed. His head would slowly droop forward and then jerk upright. We were on the center seat facing him. Suddenly he spoke. "We need to bring the fish to this boat." He closed his eyes and began to chant . . . a slow, steady, guttural chant. Greg and I looked at each other, unsure of what to make of this strange song. Dad's voice became louder, and he repeated the chant over and over again, slowly rocking his upper body with the rhythm.

Both poles bent with the strike at the same time. The drags screamed in unison and the line peeled from the reels. "Fish on!" I yelled. Greg yelled right after me, "Me too!" I could feel the great power of the fish. My pole bent almost at mid-rod, and once again I envisioned myself riding that new bike. When I got the fish close to the boat, he turned. I held the tip high and let the fish make his run. Then as quick as the strike, both of our lines went limp, and the drags fell silent. There would be no new bike. The fish were gone. They had straightened out the rusty hooks.

16 | Mr. Rettig

MR. RETTIG WAS THE LOCAL BARBER IN SUQUAMISH, AND HE VIRTUALLY owned the entire heart of the downtown area. He was, needless to say, relatively wealthy and had purchased the land from the Suquamish people many years before. The Indians at the time had great difficulty with the idea of a man owning the land. The lifetime of any man is fleeting at best. Many fathers and many sons for thousands of years have walked on the land and then perished. The Indians thought it very strange that the White men would offer to give them money for something that no one could possess. Money, on the other hand, could be exchanged for tangible merchandise, like alcohol. The exchange was willingly made. The Suquamish Reservation covered almost 8,000 acres in 1864. Today, the reservation covers less than 2,500 acres with only 73 acres being tribal land.

Mr. Rettig had a small boat equipped with an outboard motor that he kept in his boathouse on Agate Pass. He was a fisherman from the top of his head to the tip of his toes. Every night during the summer, at exactly five o'clock, he would hang the "Closed" sign in the window of his barbershop. The locals who frequented the downtown area could be seen checking the accuracy of their timepieces based on his afternoon departure. Mr. Rettig carried his fiberglass pole balanced in one hand, and his tackle box, held firmly in the other hand, would swing like a pendulum with the rhythm of his gait.

Mr. Rettig would walk down to the water, place his gear in his boat, and slowly motor out to his favorite spot. He sat by himself in the stern and fish, trolling back and forth parallel to the beach. Occasionally he would fish in an S-shaped pattern, and his nightly ritual would never vary from those two techniques.

Jim Halverson and I were tight. We were good fishing buddies. When one of us caught a fish, we would react together like a well-oiled machine. Jim was a White kid who lived several houses down from me. He owned his own boat, and the two of us regularly fished Agate Passage. We would head out in the late afternoon and return at dusk, often with little more than an empty cooler to show for our efforts. Mr. Rettig, on the other hand, would inevitably pull into his boathouse with two or three nice salmon.

The discrepancy did not go unnoticed. Jim and I, armed with an old pair of binoculars, subjected Mr. Rettig to intense scrutiny. We hid in bushes and perched in the trees. We studied his every move, and yet we could find nothing in Mr. Rettig's technique that differed from what we were doing. We used the same bait, let out the same amount of line, fished at the same time, in the same place, and trolled at the same speed. We knew that Mr. Rettig must have been doing something special that gave him an edge.

One day I decided that I could stand it no longer. A more direct approach was in order. I showed up outside of the barbershop at ten minutes to five and waited by the door. At exactly five o'clock the "Closed" sign was placed in the window, and Mr. Rettig, fishing pole and tackle box in hand, walked out the barbershop door and locked it behind him.

I followed close behind as he walked down the path to his boathouse. "Excuse me, Mr. Rettig," I said. "I was wondering if I could ask you a couple of questions?" Mr. Rettig continued walking.

"What's your name, son?" he asked without slowing or looking back.

"Emerson George, sir," I replied. Mr. Rettig stopped and turned around.

"Well, Mr. Emerson George," he said, smiling. "What can I possibly do for you?"

I was never one to hold my tongue, so I took full advantage of this invitation and proceeded to subject Mr. Rettig to an endless barrage of questions. "Well, sir," I said, "how much weight are you using? How much line do you let out? How do you cut your herring? Would you mind showing us how you tie and bait your hooks? Can me and my friend Jim follow you around so we can catch fish too?"

Mr. Rettig looked down at me, shook his head, and chuckled. "Whoa, kid," he said, "slow down. I'll tell you what. You and your friend Jim may follow me if you must." With that he loaded his gear, pushed off, and motored out to his spot. I ran back to Jim's house as fast as my short, stubby little legs would carry me.

Jim and I showed up ten minutes early every day and sat on the bench just outside the barbershop. For weeks we followed Mr. Rettig and copied his every move. We used the same weight. We used the same size hooks. We cut-plug our herring the same way. We even trolled in his wake at the same speed. Mr. Rettig would catch two or three salmon, and we would get skunked.

One evening there was no breeze and the water was like glass. Jim was not at home, so I wandered down to the beach and sat by myself listening to the myriad of sounds that carried for miles across the still water. I closed my eyes and smiled. I could hear the seagulls and a flock of geese as they flew over in formation. I could hear a chainsaw in the distance and children playing on the opposite shore. Then I heard a sound in the distance . . . an unmistakably familiar sound. It was a sound that I hadn't heard for a long time. It was a sound that I recognized; yet I just couldn't place it. I closed my eyes tighter and concentrated. The sound was getting louder. Then it came to me. "I know that sound! I know what that sound is!" I said out loud. I opened my eyes and turned toward the source. I watched and listened as a lone man and his boat slowly trolled up the channel in an S-pattern. It was Mr. Rettig . . . he was calling the fish to his boat. Mr. Rettig knew my dad's song.

17 | Sing It from the Heart

MANY YEARS LATER TWO OF MY NEPHEWS, JASON AND RODDY, arrived from Las Vegas. Jason, the oldest boy, is the son of my sister-in-law. Roddy, several years younger than Jason, is the son of my niece. Both of the boys were from broken homes, and they had no fatherly image to look up to.

One morning I called them to the kitchen table and asked them if they wanted to go fishing the following morning for sea-run, cutthroat trout. They jumped up and down with excitement. Fishing was always a good idea, and Roddy figured that anything called a "cutthroat" had to be very cool.

I grabbed my tackle box and removed a box of sharp hooks and some leader. The boys slid into chairs and stared with wide-eyed wonder as I threaded the eye of the hook, twisted the main line around the shank, wrapped the end of the line six times around the main line, and then threaded it back through the hole, pulling it tight. "Jason," I said.

"Yes, Uncle?"

"Find me a piece of cardboard for holding these sharp hooks, and I will show you boys how to tie this special knot."

I owned a little fourteen-foot Livingston at the time, and the next morning the three of us headed down the path to the water. The boys ran ahead, laughing and shoving each other. I loaded the gear in the boat, and we pushed off from the beach to fish for cutthroat trout . . . catch and release.

I headed the boat down toward Point Bolin on the southwest corner of Agate

Pass where many people were fishing. The poles were rigged up with little buzz bombs, and the hooks we had tied the night before were razor sharp. "Watch the water now," I said. "Watch the water, and when you see the fish, cast your buzz bomb in front of them and the fish will take the lure."

I sat in the back of the boat, my right hand on the throttle. The boys sat on the center seat facing me. We fished for about twenty minutes. The action was slow. "We need to bring the fish to this boat," I said. I closed my eyes and began to chant. The boys looked at each other and back at me, unsure what to make of this strange song.

I repeated the chant over and over again, slowly rocking my upper body with the rhythm. I cast my line and my pole bent with the strike of the cutthroat. "Uncle," Roddy said, eyes as big as saucers, "what is that song?"

I leaned closer and looked him in the eye. "Sing it," I said. "Sing it, Roddy, and you will catch the fish."

Jason chuckled, but I could see that Roddy believed. He closed his eyes and mimicked the chant, slowly rocking back and forth, and his pole soon bent with a nice cutthroat trout. Roddy and I continued to sing the song as fish after fish took our lures. Jason was not happy. He was getting a little disturbed. "How come I'm not catching any fish?" he complained.

"Jason," I said, "you're not singing the song."

Jason half-heartedly repeated the chant, but the fish did not come to his pole. "I sang that stupid song," he snapped. "How come I'm not catching anything now?"

I leaned toward the boy and looked him in the eye. "It is because your heart and your spirit aren't in the song," I explained. "The fish do not listen to you, Jason. Sing it like you mean it. Sing it from your heart, Jason, and you will call the fish to your hook." Jason knew that he was too old to believe in these things, but he could see in my eyes that I believed in the song. Soon the chant came to him and the fish took his bait.

I will always remember Mr. Rettig, the rusty hooks, and the power of my father's song. I know that if you sing from your heart your needs will be taken care of, and though you may not always find success, it is the way to prepare yourself, and it applies to everything you do.

18 | Hard Times

MY DAD WORKED A MYRIAD OF JOBS TO SUPPORT OUR FAMILY. Steady employment was difficult to find. He was a hard-working man who would give a solid eight hours' work for eight hours' pay. He was also a hard-drinking man, and his paychecks would often be short the standard deduction for booze. Dad did a stint working for Uncle Sam right after the Second World War at the Puget Sound Naval Shipyard in Bremerton, Washington. He was an on-call laborer for the rigging shop and would go in to work whenever he was needed. He quit that job when they asked him to pay a monthly stipend to the Veterans Association, arguing that he had paid more than his fair share of dues on the beaches and in the jungles of Okinawa. Besides, there was always other work to be had, and during the slow months he could supplement his income by picking brush, fishing, logging, and digging clams, as I've said before.

With or without money, four days after Christmas 1959 was a special day at our house. Mom and Dad were celebrating their 10th wedding anniversary, and the morning mood was festive. Mom was proudly wearing a new blue dress, and she had made a special cake. Uncle Cees had dropped by the day before with a fresh slab of elk. Dad planned to head over to Grandma's property early in the day and spend a few hours logging off a piece of land, and then that evening we were going to have a fine feast.

I was sitting in the kitchen that morning when Dad brought in a load of wood. He was out late the night before, most likely visiting Shady Rest, and his clothes were crumpled and his hair was sticking up in several directions. He stoked the fire so it would be good and hot before he headed off for Grandma's. I watched him as he squatted down on his haunches in front of the open stove and warmed his hands. That memory is very vivid for me. The glow from the fire reflected off his face, and his silhouette seemed to radiate in the flickering light. His powerful arms and barrel chest made him seem invincible, and I remember feeling secure and protected. I loved my father, and I needed nothing more than for him to say he loved me in return. He finally did . . . the night before he died.

Out on Grandma's property that morning, several trees had already been felled. Dad had just finished cutting the top off one of them and had walked down to limb the trunk end. The tree he was standing over was lying like a teeter-totter across a smaller tree with the trunk end down. The cat skinner dropped a large tree right across the topped end, and the whole business caught Dad and tossed him like a rag doll sixty feet into the air.

He landed sitting down with this right leg behind him at ninety degrees. Then he fell backwards, breaking his back. His upper leg bone was sticking out the front of his leg and had pierced the fabric of his raingear. He spent nine months in Harrison Hospital in a full body cast, immobile and in great pain.

We were in a difficult financial situation. Mom pleaded for assistance from the federal government. "My boys need shoes and clothes," she pleaded. They told her that there was nothing that could be done. These were very hard times. With Dad laid up, there was little money, even for necessities. It was the only time I ever saw my mom cry.

Poverty taught us the true meaning of "waste not, want not." Everything was used. Grandma told Greg and me that the ends of a loaf of bread were the best part. Grandma had a large garden so there were always potatoes. And in the spring and summer, fresh carrots, corn, green beans and squash would fill our stomach. My uncles would regularly bring us fresh venison and seafood.

School shopping consisted of a visit to the Salvation Army store where Greg and I would each get two pairs of pants, two shirts, and one pair of boots for school. The boots were expected to last until spring when we would each get a pair of Keds tennis shoes. I got a pair of combat boots for my first year in junior high school. They were two sizes too big and had two leather straps across the front where they laced up and tied. My mom told me that the boots were two sizes too large to allow for growth.

Several weeks before the Fourth of July, a bunch of us were lighting firecrackers at Grandma's house. Occasionally, a firecracker would not explode. We called those firecrackers fizzles. We used to break them in half and light the exposed black powder, and the fizzler would send out a hissing shower of sparks. It was common practice to light a fizzler and then quickly stomp on it. The sudden compression would result in a loud explosion. I stomped on a fizzler once while wearing my combat boots, and it blew the heel clean off. That was the last time I ever stepped on a fizzler. I found a way to patch up my boot until I got my annual pair of tennis shoes.

I knew I was poor, but I never felt poor until that first year in junior high school. For some reason, between the sixth and seventh grade, being "cool" became the prime directive. Maybe it's the rut . . . posturing and preening to attract a mate . . . Mother Nature's way of prolonging the species . . . being cool and attractive and accepted. Whatever the motivation, cruelty at this time of life is practiced with great abandon.

My first day in junior high school was relatively uneventful. My second day wasn't bad either, until I ran into one of my cousins in wood shop who informed me, loud enough for all to hear, that I was wearing that same shirt that I had worn the day before. The two shirts in my closet were always clean; there just wasn't much to choose from. It was the first time I felt the pain of class distinction.

I dug clams commercially for money to help the family. I had been digging commercially since I was ten. I never made a lot of money, but it was a way for me to contribute. I would get my Christmas money digging clams. I remember one night in November. Dad and I were down on the beach, elbow deep in a clam hole. The Coleman lantern was hanging from a bent crook in a piece of rebar we had driven into the sand. Digging for clams is done at low tide, and when the tide changes and starts to come in, the clam hole is quickly flooded and the clam-digging window of opportunity is short-lived, so digging fast and furious is the accepted technique. That night there were schools of squid that were attracted to the light of the hissing lantern. I scooped up dozens of squid with my clam fork and tossed them behind us up onto the beach. When the tide turned and covered the clam beds, it was time to gather our buckets of clams, pick up the squid and call it a night. When we stood, to our great surprise, we discovered that it had been snowing the entire time and a half-inch of wet snow coated our backs.

There is a smell on the beach . . . a smell of salt water and barnacles . . . a smell that comes from digging clams . . . a smell that cannot be removed with soap and water. In junior high I realized that only the poor Indian kids smelled like clams. The White kids didn't. I was aware of the fact that my family and my ancestors harvested clams for subsistence, and I remained fiercely proud of that heritage, but the smell of clams suddenly became the scent of poverty, and I deeply resented the implication. I no longer thought I was poor . . . I knew it . . . and there was an endless supply of kids at school who were quick to remind me of my place.

I got in a lot fistfights with kids who taunted me about my clothes or my smell. I was particularly upset with one of my cousins who, to save face, emphatically denied he was Indian. He is now hardcore Indian complete with shoulder braids down his back, but in school he and I were at odds because he denied his heritage.

I saved my class pictures from the first grade through the fifth grade. I still have them. My sixth grade photograph was the first year that school pictures were printed in color. I was selected by my teacher that year to hold the class sign that said Mr. Stoke's Sixth Grade Class. I proudly sat in the front with my legs crossed and the placard on my lap. When the pictures arrived I couldn't wait to see how I looked holding the sign. I opened the package and pulled out the photograph. Several of the kids in my class made fun of me. I was the only kid in the picture with holes in my jeans. I tore that photograph into tiny pieces.

On May 19, 1963, I was walking alone to the bus stop. It was a nice, calm, spring day. I walked past the new grade school and stopped. Mrs. Johnson, the school janitor, lived on the other side of the street from the school. The sidewalk in front of her house had always lined up perfectly with the old school flagpole that was still there. I looked down in front of me and saw that there was a chunk of asphalt out of the road. As I stepped over that hole I made a pledge to myself that I would always remember that step. There was no particular reason . . . just an idealistic impulse of youth.

I was right though. To this very day I clearly remember that moment. When I got home that evening, my mom, Greg, and I cried, pleaded, and begged for my dad to remove the loaded pistol from his mouth.

19 | Eye to Eye

I HUNG AROUND WITH SEVERAL OTHER INDIAN KIDS AT SCHOOL. I suppose it was important at that age to belong to a clique . . . a circle of friends with whom you shared some commonality. I ate lunch with Charlie George, my second cousin, and George Sparks, a distant kin. Both of them were from the Little Boston Indian Reservation.

After lunch, the three of us usually headed for the gym to shoot baskets, or we would sneak off limits behind the building to just shoot the shit or play mumblety-peg. Mumblety-peg involved the art of balancing the point of a knife on your fingertip and then flipping the knife in the air where it must then complete three rotations and stick in the ground. If successful, the launching pad would be moved to another part of the anatomy, such as the elbow or toe. These games were always competitive and spirited, though the true purpose of our secret gatherings was to simply find solace and camaraderie in each other's company.

One day we were involved in a lively game of mumblety-peg when around the corner of the building stepped the vice-principal. There was no more frightening an apparition than our vice-principal. His entire purpose in life was to inspire fear and respect and to exact a terrible vengeance on any misguided child who should dare to break a rule or cross the line. There was an authoritative vigor and sternness to his voice that would send chills down the spines of all but the bravest of the brave.

"What is it that you boys are doing back here?" he growled, suspiciously eyeing the knife.

None of us answered. Charlie and George looked down at the ground. It was apparent by the veins that bulged in the vice-principal's neck that he was not happy with the lack of response.

"I asked you boys what you are doing back here, and I want to know what you are doing with that weapon?"

Again, no one answered. Charlie and George continued to look down at the ground. I found myself studying their faces. My grandfather taught me that in traditional native culture, eye contact was a sign of disrespect.

The vice-principal was irate. "You boys look at me when I'm talking to you!" he yelled. Charlie and George reacted instinctively, their eyes still cast to the ground. The vice-principal was livid. "I told you boys to look at me when I'm . . . "

I stepped in front of my cousins and looked up at the dreaded administrator, and a fire burned in my heart. "You do not know who we are!" I yelled. "You do not know who we are!" The vice-principal was temporarily taken aback. "I am Emerson George, and we were playing mumblety-peg. That is all we were doing. We were just playing mumblety-peg. We weren't doing anything wrong!"

The vice-principal quickly regained his composure and glared down at me. His eyes narrowed and his knurly index finger bobbed like a cork in my face. "Don't you use that tone of voice with me, young man," he scolded. "Who do you think you're talking to?" The question, I assumed, was rhetorical, and I stood my ground. There was no need to respond. I was suddenly well aware of the answer.

Observing Charlie and George, and their actions, was a significant event in my life. From that day forward I knew that I must cross the cultural boundary. I must be one to stand up and speak for those who are unable. I must be one with the courage to look an adversary or antagonist in the eye and stand firm. As for the unauthorized game of mumblety-peg, the three of us were summarily punished.

20 | Journey to Discovery

OVER ONE HUNDRED AND TEN YEARS AGO, NO WHITE MAN HAD EVER set foot in the interior of the Olympic Mountain Range. In November of 1889, Elisha Ferry, then governor of the Territory of Washington scheduled a press conference. He announced to a room full of reporters that it was time to clear up the mystery that surrounded the unexplored interior of the Olympic Mountain Range. This was a very big deal. The city of Seattle was full of entrepreneurs, from fur trappers to miners to lumbermen, who could just taste the money to be made from such a large tract of untapped natural resources.

The governor continued his address by retelling a story that had been shared around countless campfires by both Indians and non-Indians. In an earlier time, as the legend went, a remote valley had existed. The valley was a paradise where the Indians gathered for potlatches. A potlatch is an Indian festival . . . party time, where games are played and gifts and pleasantries are exchanged. It was in this valley that some terrible disaster had occurred and many Indians were killed. The few that escaped were too afraid to ever return. Indians and non-Indians alike truly feared the area and few would consider traveling to the interior.

The governor told of the possibility of a large lake formed by the drainage of the mountain glaciers. He explained to the members of the press that he felt it imperative for a White man to find this hidden valley, plow up the sweet grasses and wild flowers, and raise crops and livestock. Such a fine opportunity to cash in on paradise must have truly been hard to resist.

The governor's challenge to local explorers made the papers the next day. The *Seattle Press* newspaper promised fame and glory to the first explorer to go where no White man had ever been. Now, this all sounds a wee bit silly today, especially since hundreds of thousands of people now enjoy the many campgrounds, trails, lakes and rivers of Olympic National Park. But don't forget that in 1889 there were no maps, no charts, no aerial photographs, no personal computers, no satellite imagery, no maintained trails, no aluminum-framed packs or Coleman camp stoves, no flashlights or sleeping bags, no Global Positioning Satellites, no ranger cabins, and no freeze-dried eggs. There weren't even any toasters. There was nothing but a vast unknown, a place of wonder and mystery where an ancient legend told of a great disaster. There were very few takers.

The *Seattle Press* did receive a letter from a guy named Christie from North Yakima. Mr. Christie wrote that he was prepared to venture into the unknown, but he had insufficient funds to properly outfit his expedition. The *Seattle Press* was impressed with Christie's credentials and agreed to provide financial backing. Christie's exploration of the Olympic Mountains would come to be known as the Press Expedition.

Christie was a man fit for the task. He was a rugged and sturdy Scotsman in his thirties. He dressed in hunter's garb, and his long, curly hair was usually tied with a headband worn Indian style. Christie carried his rifle under his arm, and he traveled with two bear dogs that he called Bud and Tweed.

Christie assembled a party of five men: John W. Simms was a trader, hunter, trapper and prospector who had fought in the Boer War; John Henry Crumback, at only thirty-three, was an old Indian fighter who knew how to handle himself in the mountains; Christopher O'Connell Hayes was the grandson of the great Irish liberal, Daniel O'Connell; Dr. Harry Boyle Runnalls of Puyallup would accompany the party as physician; and Captain Charles A. Barnes, a friend of Christie's and an experienced mountain explorer, would travel with the team as topographer.

The expedition took a steamer to Port Angeles. Their plan was to enter the Olympics through the valley of the Elwha River. Mr. Norman Smith, a so-called expert on the Elwha and the self-proclaimed mayor of Port Angeles, told the men that the river was navigable for over thirty miles. Based on this information, Christie and his men camped by the river for weeks and built a boat that they christened *Gertie*. Hundred of pounds of supplies were stowed aboard her in preparation for the journey. On the evening before they were to depart, the men had a wonderful feast of fish and game. The celebration lasted late into the evening, and the mood was festive. There was great anticipation and excitement, for their weeks of planning and preparation were finally coming to an end.

Christie awoke early the next morning. He was restless. He walked to the river and squatted down on his haunches in the deep snow. The water was ice cold and milk-colored. His breath condensed in the cool air. He could see piles of fresh elk droppings still steaming on the far bank. "Today is the day," he thought to himself. He reached up and pulled the collar of his wool coat tightly around his neck and smiled. He removed his journal from its pouch on his hip and made an entry: 13 January 1890 . . . Today we began our journey upriver.

It's probably a good thing for Mr. Norman Smith that he was safe and warm back in Port Angeles, for the Press Expedition found little that was navigable about the Elwha. Remember that there was no dam and no Mills Lake, and the lower stretches of the river were wild and dangerous. Huge boulders, rapids, fallen trees, and swift currents barred the way. For ten days the men waded through frigid, glacial waters and fought the swirling current. They only managed to travel less than six miles. Frustrated and exhausted, they tied *Gertie* to a tree and went on by foot.

For the next three days it snowed heavily and then rained. It was impossible to travel. The men were forced to wait two weeks for the weather to clear. The Press Expedition, rested and fed, struggled onward through the underbrush and over fallen trees. Fortunately there was no shortage of food. The river teemed with salmon and trout. The deer were so plentiful and tame that Barnes complained in his diary that it was no sport to hunt. This was indeed a paradise. Crumback pledged to return to this place and homestead. The men helped him cut trees and lay the foundation for his future cabin. Nearby, Crumback blazed a fir to indicate that this was his claim. On the other side of the fir he marked the three horizontal blazes of the Press Expedition. The blazes were spaced about a foot apart.

The men soon found evidence that supported the stories of Indians once roaming the mountains and having potlatches. They discovered tree blazes along what appeared to be an old Indian trail. The blazes were at least two hundred years old. They also found wringing posts that the Indians used to cure skins. The posts were so old that they seemed ready to crumble if touched. One day they came upon a steep landslide area where it appeared as though the whole mountain had collapsed into the valley. They recalled the legend of a tremendous catastrophe that had killed so many Indians, and they named the place Convolution Canyon.

The Press Expedition explored the interior of the Olympic Mountains for almost six months before returning to Seattle. They developed topographical maps of the terrain and documented the abundance of flora and fauna, but more importantly, they put to rest the persistent legends of danger and mystery. Today the hike up the Elwha to the Low and High Divide, across the skyline trail, and down the North Fork of the Quinault River can be done in less than a week. Tens of thousands have made the journey. Teddy Roosevelt hiked the trail and surely hunted the plentiful game and fished in pools full of trout. John and Bobby Kennedy and their families hiked up the Elwha. I was told that the shelters at Elkhorn Camp were built specifically to accommodate the Kennedy party. Walt Disney took his camera crew up the Elwha to film a documentary on the Olympic elk. I remember seeing the movie when I was a kid.

The Press Expedition left a legacy for those who have traveled up the Elwha from the trailhead at Whiskey Bend. Mr. Christie and his men named many of the landmarks: The Lillian River, Mary's Falls, Hayes River, Lake Mary, and Lake Margaret. The hiking trail is well marked and well maintained. Bridges have been built to ford rushing mountain streams, and switchback trails ease the passage over rough terrain.

I've probably hiked up every river that drains from the Olympic Mountains except for the Bogachiel and the Sol Duc. I am very comfortable in the wilderness. All of these trips were memorable, but there was one journey I will always remember.

I was excited and very proud when I was selected by the Olympic Scouting Council to represent my troop on a 66-mile hike over the Olympics. It was the summer of 1965, and I had anticipated the journey for months. A car caravan of parents and Scouts wound their way north and westward through Chimacum and Sequim, towns that bear Indian names. The Elwha River Valley is a dozen miles west of Port Angeles. There is a park road that winds its way along the river to the trailhead at Whiskey Bend. It took the Press Expedition weeks to travel that far.

We piled out of the cars in a rush of activity. Camping gear was unloaded from the vehicles and placed on the ground. Packs were checked and rechecked. We took turns lifting each other's pack so our arms could easily be slipped through the shoulder slings. I was saddled with the fifteen-pound cast iron cooking griddle, so I promptly ate all of my cookies and trail mix hoping to eliminate as much weight as possible. Scoutmaster Orville Schultz took a head count. Fifty teenage boys laughed, whooped, and hollered in anticipation. Mr. Schultz barked instructions. "Quiet boys! Listen up now!" he bellowed. "I want you all to stay together. Form a line in single file. When we are all ready, we will head up the trail. Our first camp will be at an old homestead called Hume's Ranch. Remember, boys," he paused, scanning the eager faces of his young charges, all eyes looking in his direction, "this journey starts with the first step." With that, he turned and we fell in behind. The entire procession headed up the trail in military fashion. The great adventure had begun.

We arrived at Hume's Ranch in the late afternoon. It was a trek of several miles from the trailhead. We all went about setting up camp. I was grateful to remove the weight of the dreaded griddle from my back. I leaned my pack against a tree and set up my plastic-sheet tent. There were several hours of daylight left, and I was anxious to finally see the river. I grabbed my fishing pole and headed off through the brush. Everywhere I looked I found deer and elk tracks. I knelt down and gently ran my fingers through a fresh elk print in the soft, moist earth and smiled. For me, this was a good sign. When I came to the river I was surprised at how fast the water swirled and rushed downstream. There were numerous large rocks that deflected the flow, and I knew that in the pools formed on the backside of these rocks I would find large trout.

There was a huge boulder right in front of the ranch that jutted into the river. I found a foothold and climbed the face of the rock. The boulder was flat on top, and I found I could lie down with little worry of falling into the river. I flopped on my belly and watched large fish skirting the rapids. A deep pool of crystal clear water bubbled on the downstream side, and I could see the fish effortlessly glide from side to side over the sandy bottom. The musical drone of the river filled my ears. The sun warmed my back and the cool misty air filled my lungs. I could feel the magic in this place.

Around the campfire that night Mr. Schultz told the story of the Press Expedition. We all sat in a circle and listened intently to a tale of exploration and adventure. Mr. Schultz explained that many of the places we would visit in the coming days were named by the members of the Press Expedition. He told how Christie and his men reportedly marked, or blazed, their trail by slashing three horizontal grooves in the sides of trees. He told us to keep an eye out for these trail blazes, for in the seventy-five years that had passed since the expedition, none had ever been found.

Early the next morning the camp was bustling with activity. Several campfires were started, and we all gathered around the flames for warmth against the morning chill. Anyone who has ever gone hiking and camping in the mountains will tell you that fresh air and exercise make for a healthy appetite, and feeding a ravenous pack of hungry boys was a major undertaking. The cast iron griddle that I had reluctantly transported to the campsite had suddenly become a very good friend, now that its flat surface was home to a half dozen fat, brown pancakes.

After breakfast we all rolled up our sleeping bags and loaded our packs. It was decided that the group would split into two parties. The instructions were for everyone to meet in a certain spot at a predetermined time where lunch would be prepared. I listened well and I understood. I knew that to stay on course I must keep the sound of the river on my right, so several of us teamed up and set out early.

I had always found solace in the woods. Among the trees and the animals I felt at home. I had learned as a small boy to use my eyes and ears, and I found that the forest filled my senses. I could hear voices in the constant drone of the river. The chatter of the ground squirrels and the rhythm of the woodpecker seemed to reassure me. The call of the raven was a sound I had always found refreshing. In the woods I was at peace.

The others seemed to be in a headlong rush against time. They knew there were many miles of switchbacks between where they stood and the day's camp. The destination was their focus and so the destination was all that mattered. Squarehead's little brother, Danny Olson, and I lingered behind. I had learned a lesson from my grandpa that, like Joe Hilliar and the totem pole, there was great joy to be found in the journey. An eagle soared above the trees when I looked. A coyote howled in the deep woods when I listened. All along the trail we found bush after bush of plump, sweet blueberries, and Danny and I took our time consuming handfuls of the juicy fruit.

We found our way along the main trail that skirted the Elwha. I spotted a deep, green swirling hole in the river below that I knew would be teeming with trout.

Danny and I removed our packs and climbed down a steep embankment. That was the day I learned about periwinkles. Danny showed me how to remove the worm-like larvae from its home of sticks and use it to bait my hook. Periwinkles seemed to be the hot ticket, and the two of us fished, catch and release, until our arms were tired.

Danny and I shouldered our packs and continued down the trail. We soon arrived at the place that had been selected for lunch break. There was a lot of anxiety and confusion among the leaders. The second party had not shown up as scheduled and the adults were very concerned. After lunch, word was put out that we would all stay together and continue on to that night's camping site where we would wait to hopefully rendezvous with the missing group.

That evening campsite was well away from the river. While the adults huddled in concerned discussion, I headed down to the river where I found myself standing on the edge of a cliff. It was nearly a vertical drop down to the water. I looked around but there was no way to climb down, so I picked huckleberries instead. When I got back to camp I put up a lean-to tent over my sleeping bag with a piece of plastic, some twine, shower hooks, and rocks and spent the rest of the afternoon feasting on blueberries.

Hours passed, darkness fell, and there was no sign of the other party. The mood in camp turned very dark. Though not far from the trailhead, the area between Hume's Ranch and the second campsite was crisscrossed with hundreds of animal trails, some of which ended in abrupt ledges with sheer cliffs that dropped hundreds of feet into boiling rapids.

The adults decided to send back runners to try and find the missing party. Mr. Schultz selected two boys who had run track for Bainbridge Island. They headed off for Hume's Ranch searching side trails and stopping to call out along the way. The seventeen missing team members were nowhere to be found. Mr. Schultz instructed the runners that if they failed to find the other party, they were to go directly to the ranger station and report what had happened. The rangers immediately organized an extensive search. The next morning they called in helicopters from the Department of Natural Resources for aerial support. One of the helicopter pilots spotted the missing party later that afternoon. They were on the other side of the river high on a ridge with no trails to follow. Apparently, they had chosen a path that crossed the river and had decided that it must be the right way.

When the runners returned to camp and informed Mr. Schultz that the missing group was found, there was great relief. It was decided that we would lay over another day and wait for the missing party to catch up. The next morning the ranger showed up in camp. He told Mr. Schultz that the lost group had been instructed to make their way down to the river where they were to look for a specific landmark. At that place the water would be swift but shallow enough to make a crossing. We followed Mr. Schultz and the ranger down to the river where one of the boys was selected to ford the river carrying a rope. The rope was strung from bank to bank and the lost party used it to make their way across the river. Pictures of that portage were published in the *Bremerton Sun* newspaper.

That night the entire party celebrated the reunion. The leaders were visibly relieved, and we all reveled in the great adventure. Everything was back to normal except for our carefully planned menu, which was now all out of whack. The lost party had been carrying all of the potatoes and, finding themselves with little else to eat, had consumed most of our spuds. It was decided that living off the land, which was second nature to me, would be the only way to make up for our food shortages. We feasted on powdered eggs for breakfast with extra sustenance provided by fresh trout and wild berries. Two more trout breakfasts and one trout dinner and the menu was back on track.

One evening Danny, Jim Sergeant, another boy from Bremerton, and I grabbed our fishing gear and headed up the trail in search of a fishing hole. We crossed a little creek that cut through the main trail and trickled down through the brush. I knew that where this little drink of water dumped into the river there would be good fishing. We worked our way down the creek. We came out through the brush onto the edge of a cliff that was about thirty feet above the river. The bank on the other side was about fifteen feet off the water, and standing alone in the middle of the far bank was an old hemlock tree. We were discussing our options, and then one by one fell silent, staring in disbelief at the gnarled trunk of the hemlock. Fifteen to twenty feet up was the aged and scarred-over triple blaze of the Press Expedition. The Press Expedition traveled up the Elwha River in the dead of winter. The blazes were right where they put them on the trunk of a tree . . . while they were standing in ten feet of snow. Nobody could find the Press Expedition trail-blazes because they never looked up. We proudly reported the discovery of the blazes to the National Park Service and the Department of Natural Resources.

We broke camp the next day and headed away from the river toward the alpine country. We passed an old-growth tree that stood by itself alongside the trail, and I remember wondering how many centuries that tree had stood and what significant historical events had occurred during its lifetime. We climbed a series of grueling switchbacks that led to the High Divide where we made camp. A dozen of us decided to hike up Mt. Seattle. I got to within a 100 feet of the summit. The last stretch was nearly vertical and, not being that fond of heights, I watched as one of the other boys climbed to the top and thrust his arms in the air in victory. I preserved the moment with a photograph.

It was a crystal-clear day, and from the flank of Mt. Seattle I could look in all directions and see unparalleled grandeur. There was a magnificent waterfall in the distance that spilled from the top of a high mountain gorge and cascaded to the valley below. I could see the Elwha River twisting its way through the mountains and out to the Pacific. Old-growth forests grew tall in all directions. There were pristine mountain lakes and dozens of snow-capped peaks that drained to the river valleys below.

We decided that the difficult climb up the mountain was certainly deserving of some sort of reward, so we improvised sleds from our backpacks and sheets of plastic and rode our inventions down the snow fields. The ride was fast, fun and furious. On the way back to camp we discovered endless fields of blueberries. I gorged myself. I also had feasted on blueberry pancakes that morning. The blueberries exacted their revenge later that afternoon, and I spent the remainder of the evening camped out by the outhouse.

Lake Beauty was the last campsite in the high country. The next day we would drop down into the valley of the Quinault. It was easy to see how Lake Beauty got its name. There were sheer cliffs on three sides, and the deep, calm water reflected like a mirror. It was difficult to tell where that water ended and the cliffs began. We caught and released dozens of trout. The fish were very large, and we were at a loss to explain how trout could grow so huge with so little to eat.

Later that day, as the sun slowly dipped toward the horizon, I sat by myself on the shores of Lake Beauty. I was admiring the grandeur of this virtual paradise when suddenly, like some Biblical plague, a great black cloud of blood-sucking mosquitoes rose up from the water and swarmed around fifty helpless, warm-blooded mammals who scurried in all directions, arms flailing. There was no place to run and no place to hide. It was an issue of survival. I hate to sleep with my head covered but on this occasion it was the only answer. We all dove into our sleeping bags and sealed ourselves inside to keep from being sucked dry.

We woke the next morning, ate breakfast, and headed down the trail. We soon entered the Upper Quinault Valley. I gazed in wonder at the blankets of deep green moss that dripped from the branches of every tree. The air was cool and fresh, and I often closed my eyes and slowly filled my lungs. This was a magic place, a spiritual place.

As we traversed down the valley, I could see where the loggers of a hundred years ago had moved up. There were remnants of giant Douglas fir trees. Some of these ancient trees had stood over forty stories tall. Their stumps measured up to eighteen feet at the base. The springboard notches and undercuts were still visible. Many of these trees were a thousand years old when they fell to the axe. I was deeply disturbed by what I saw. I could tell where the giant firs had fallen because the entire top two-thirds of the trees still rested and rotted where they landed. I could see where the loggers fell the tree, walked to the first limb about 150 feet away, and made a second cut. That bottom portion is all that they took . . . no knots. The rest of the tree, over six feet across at the thickest end, was left to rot.

We made camp that night where the ancient forest once stood. I found a huge fallen log and placed the end of my plastic tarp on top using large rocks to hold it fast. I anchored the other end of the tarp with stakes. It was a very humbling experience for me to know that I was camped against something that ancient and sacred that was shown so little respect.

That night a cougar ran up the log above my head and screamed. There are no words to adequately describe a cougar sound. Suffice it to say that the hair stood up on the back of my neck. There were three boys who pitched there that night. Not one of us spoke, and we all found sleep very difficult.

I will always remember that journey across the Olympics, for it truly was a trail of discovery. I hiked up a wild river that teemed with trout. My friends and I found the long-sought-after trail-blazes of the Press Expedition. I climbed the Low Divide and stood in the shadow of trees that had lived for a millennium. I climbed the flanks of a mountain and scanned a panorama of unrivaled natural beauty. I had been with Sealth in the mountains, and as I traversed out of what I had come to know, I was deeply affected by the transition and the waste that I witnessed in the Valley of the Quinault. From that time forward I would have a great respect for the natural way of things, and I would be acutely aware of the environmental damage that I have witnessed in my short lifetime.

 **21 | Travesty**

CONSERVATIONISTS ESTIMATE THAT THE CURRENT EXTINCTION RATE is ten thousand times greater than it should be under normal circumstances. I call that one hell of an estimate. Over eleven thousand plants and animals are, at this very moment, teetering on the brink of extinction. Why? Humans. Too damn many of us. Expanding cities, deforestation, pollution, agriculture, ozone depletion, over-fishing, you name it. Maybe the movie *The Matrix* was right. Maybe humanity is a virus, multiplying and consuming until everything is gone.

When I was a young boy, my grandfather told me that most of the incredible bounty of the Northwest was gone long before I was even born. The devastation continues virtually unchecked. A decade or so ago you could scuba dive off the dock at Illahee State Park and at a depth of 60 feet; the bottom was literally covered by a field of large geoduck necks as far as the eye could see.

In the mid-1980s a private company sought permission from the state to selectively harvest geoducks. The Kitsap County Council, at the bidding of their constituents, refused to authorize the geoduck harvest. The people of Kitsap County indicated that they wanted the Kitsap County geoduck population preserved for the people of Kitsap County. At the same time, the county was in line for a block of state funding. The money was earmarked for the repair of severely damaged road surfaces including Highways 3 and 16 from Bremerton heading out of town through Gorst to the Belfair–Port Orchard–Tacoma junctions. These badly needed repairs were on the top of the state's priority list one day, and figuratively speaking, somewhere on page 67 the next.

The road surfaces continued to decay until, upon pleas by the citizenry for action, the County Council capitulated on the issue of commercial geoduck har-vesting. The Washington State Department of Natural Resources apparently held our county road repairs hostage. Interesting twist of fate, losing your natural resources to the Department of Natural Resources. I have always believed that natural resources be-longed to the people, Indians and non-Indians alike; however, it would appear as though our natural resources are there for the many to lose and the few to use.

At last report, there were no geoducks off the dock at Illahee. I can't speak for the numerous other underwater locations in the Puget Sound that are known to nurture the growth of these giant clams, but commercial harvesting activities by Indian and non-Indian alike tend to leave me with little hope for clams unscathed. Whatever legal and/or illegal harvesting activities that are still ongoing is anyone's guess, but whenever and wherever there is a resource worth a great deal of money, ripe for the taking, I have complete faith that the power of human greed will dic-tate commercial enterprise, and with that realization I have learned a painful les-son . . . that greed favors neither culture nor ethnicity. Indians from the Skokomish Reservation were recently caught high-grading geoducks . . . digging up every single clam and discarding all but the premium size. In January of 2001, the De-partment of Natural Resources once again strongly suggested that permission be given to harvest geoducks in Kitsap County.

Besides geoducks, sea cucumbers were found. They are underwater creatures that are shaped like their name. They have two very thin strips of meat on their undersides. They were once found in abundance in the Puget Sound and for de-cades were harvested for personal use by area divers. Not long ago sea cucumber populations were virtually decimated by commercial harvesting. They took them all. A popular Northwest restaurant used the tasty strips of meat for making imi-tation clam strips. The Japanese are also quite fond of sea cucumbers. Personally, I never had a reason to eat a sea cucumber, as they always appeared to me as large slugs, but if for some strange reason the mood should ever strike, I can always catch a flight to Japan. Please understand that I cast no aspersions toward my Asian brothers. In a free capitalist market economy, greed would dictate that the meat of the sea cucumber goes to the highest bidder.

In the mid-'70s, I fished for Pacific true cod in the Puget Sound. You could fish just about anywhere in January and February and quickly catch three or four nice-sized fish. Friends and family would gather at the George house and we would have a fresh fish fry. True cod has a firm, succulent flesh and a wonderful, mild flavor. Three or four fish would easily feed a dozen folks. The true cod are virtually gone now! They were harvested in the '80s by commercial boats that dragged their spawning grounds underneath the Agate Pass bridge. Hundreds of thousands of fish gone …wiped out! It's been over twenty years since I've seen true cod in anyone's net.

In Shelton, Washington, and in many other locations in the Northwest, there are sawmills in operation that process the trees from our forests and sell them to the Japanese. I've heard it argued that the lumber companies are growing and harvesting their own trees. I understand that many logging outfits are considerably more conscientious about forestry management than they were in the past, though I'm sadly confident that somewhere there are large, knot-free, 350-foot virgin Douglas fir trees that will soon be deprived of their 700-plus years of existence.

The South Fork of the Hoh River tumbles down from the mountains, through Olympic National Park, and into the North Fork for the remaining journey to the sea. Families used to camp in a small, maintained campground alongside a stand of ancient trees, some of which were more than ten feet in diameter. The green, glacial waters literally teemed with rainbow trout, steelhead trout and salmon. In the late '70s and early '80s, the trees were commercially harvested from high atop the ridge all the way down to the riverbank. This "selective" harvest stopped at the western boundary of the Olympic National Park only because there are those who continually fight hard to hold that line.

The winter rains fell that year and scoured great gouges into the naked sides of the mountain, sending a torrent of mud, rocks, and logging slag into river. The South Fork of the Hoh no longer curves its way through groves of birch trees, over the rocks and pebbles rounded by a millennium of tumbling water. When it rains now the river flows straight, fast, high, and muddy, interrupted only by piles of debris and logjams of ancient root-balls. In the blink of a geological eye, an entire ecosystem was devastated . . . spawning beds buried in sediment . . . deep, green holes full of salmon and trout, gone . . . a place of wondrous beauty destroyed for generations. The forest will be back—nature has a way—but chances are good that I'll be dead by then and so will you.

Every part of this country is sacred to my people.
Every hillside, every valley, every plain and grove
has been hallowed by some fond memory

or some sad experience of my tribe.
Even the rocks,
which seem to lie dumb as they swelter in the sun
along the silent shore in solemn grandeur
thrill with memories of past events
connected with the fate of my people,
the very dust under your feet
responds more lovingly to our footsteps than to yours,
because it is the ashes of our ancestors,
and our bare feet are conscious of the sympathetic touch,
for the soil is rich with the life of our kindred.

As Tribal Council Chairman, I was often invited to speak on environmental issues. At one such meeting I was speaking to a group of folks gathered to deal with the environmental damage in the Keyport Lagoon. The lagoon is a superfund site. Tons of bad stuff—lead, chromium, cadmium, you name it—was dumped into the lagoon years ago and then backfilled. I was invited to talk to that group along with several others folks, including Phyllis Meyers, a marine biologist for whom I have a great deal of respect. I was telling this group what I believed to be true, that they could gauge the health of a river or creek by whether or not the salmon come back. When I finished my presentation and sat down in my chair, Phyllis leaned toward me and whispered in my ear. "If you really want to know the health of the creek," she said, "put your hands in the gravel, get down close to the water, and look for the little critters. If there are no little critters, then the salmon will not return." I have never forgotten her words. It was a very clarifying moment for me knowing that life depends on the survival of the little things.

Many of our wild Northwest rivers were dammed in the last century—most notably, the Columbia, the Elwha, and the Snake. The dams stopped the natural flow of those rivers and created huge lakes that flooded Indian fishing grounds. The countless salmon that once journeyed hundreds of miles inland to lay their eggs and die were blocked from their spawning grounds. Several species of salmon have recently been classified as endangered, and many prominent politicians have spoken out in support of removing the dams as a way to save the resource. It is foolish to deny that there are two sides to the coin. Dams provide hydroelectric power. The lakes formed behind some of those dams provide recreation as well as irrigation for the eastern half of Washington state, turning what was an arid wasteland into fertile farmland. The dams also slow the flow of the mighty Columbia, allowing the lower stretches of the river to serve as a vital highway for commerce.

So, how do we get the salmon past the dams to their spawning grounds upriver? The fact is that the salmon do make it past the dams, either by way of fish ladders or by literally being scooped up and transported. The salmon getting up the river to spawn has never been an insurmountable problem. The real problem is the inability of the baby salmon, or smolt, to make their way back to the ocean without being chewed to pieces in the turbines that generate our electricity and control the water levels. Before the dams, the salmon would spawn and the smolt would ride the fast river currents down to the ocean. The entire journey took five to seven days. Today, the baby salmon meander through the lakes behind the dams and many of them eventually get sucked into the turbines.

I propose that we go to the headwaters of the Snake River and build a fish slide down to the ocean. Loggers used to make log flumes. They would tap into a stream or creek, build a trough, and throw the log into the trough. The water in the trough would send the log down to the main river where it would float to the mill. That idea is very similar to the chutes at today's water parks where kids slide down a stream of water that runs through a series of long tubes. We could find a survey showing the elevations of the original Snake River streambed and build a water slide for the smolt that duplicates the original river bottom . . . create pools for them to rest in. If they were to occasionally tumble over an eight-foot waterfall on the way down, I believe it would make for a hardier fish.

Stainless steel or Plexiglas guides with holes in them would direct the smolt into the tube before the turbines or, better yet, just spawn them up river and dump them into the slide. The chute would only be pulling thirty-six inches of water off the river by its length, which is nothing. The Columbia River Alliance, which represents navigation, electrical utilities, forest products, industry, agriculture, and other river-user groups would not be impacted. Our dwindling salmon stocks would return to the river by the hundreds of thousands. Expensive? Perhaps! But the revenue from the enhanced recreational fishery alone would surely offset the cost of construction.

22 | The Price of Freedom

MY TRUE POTENTIAL WAS NEVER REALIZED DURING THOSE EARLY, formative years. I managed to complete my education at North Kitsap High School in Poulsbo. I graduated with the class of 1968. The war in Vietnam was in full swing. You could count the choices for a healthy eighteen-year-old boy on one hand: Vietnam, Canada, or college. For me, fleeing the country was never an option. I was raised in a very patriotic family. The American flag was proudly displayed on the front of our house. I believed, with ever fiber of my being, that there was a price to be paid for our freedom. I still believe that. I'm just not sure anymore what that price should be.

High school graduation exercises were scheduled for June 4. I had enlisted in the Coast Guard and was scheduled to report to boot camp in Alameda, California, on June 2. My high school annual even had the words "Future U.S. Coast Guard" under my name. There was only one slight problem—the graduating senior keg party on May 19. The party was up and running at full speed when the Kitsap County Sheriff showed up for the celebration. He didn't arrest anybody for drinking, but he did remove the keg. He even topped off my beer on the way out. He even offered us some free advice: "You boys be careful driving home tonight."

The party ended shortly after the keg was removed . . . no beer, no party. I walked out to my car that was parked at the end of the road, hopped inside, and drove home. Unbeknownst to me, the sheriff had written down the license plate numbers of every car. A week later I received a 3 x 5 postcard in the mail. It stated, in plain English, that I had been seen at a party where there was minor consumption of alcohol and the United States Coast Guard was no longer interested in my services.

I immediately took a trip down to the Air Force Recruiting Station. I entered the building and found a man in uniform sitting behind a large wooden desk. The man seemed more than happy to see me. "Can I help you, son?" he said, pointing at the lone chair that sat in front of his desk. "Please have a seat." I sat.

"Yes, Sir," I said, "I want to join up."

"Excellent, son! Have you taken our entrance test?"

I squirmed. "Well, yeah, kinda," I said. "You guys came to my school awhile back and took me out of class and gave me your test. I marked all of the answers 'D' because I was planning on joining the Coast Guard."

They let me retake the test. They compared the two grades and couldn't believe I was the same guy they had tested months earlier. I was in the United States Air Force as of May 15, 1969. Boot camp was at Blackman Air Force Base in San Antonio, Texas. From there I was stationed at Chinook Field in Illinois . . . sixty miles south of Chicago. I had a cousin who lived in Chicago with her husband. She and I were born on the same day, and we had always shared a special camaraderie. I called her from the base to say hi and to let her know I was in the area. She invited me over to the house for a visit. "Catch a Greyhound," she said, "and I'll pick you up at the bus station when you arrive."

I hopped a Greyhound Trailways bus and arrived in Chicago feeling very proud and looking quite impressive in my pressed Air Force uniform and shiny, patent-leather shoes. Traffic was light and the bus had made excellent time, arriving about fifteen minutes earlier than scheduled. I looked around for my cousin, but she hadn't arrived yet, so I grabbed myself a seat on a nearby bench . . . back straight, chest out.

There was a little old lady sitting across from me and I smiled at her and nodded. The old woman got up from her seat and walked over to where I was sitting. I looked up at her and smiled.

"Hello, " I said, "I'm Emerson George. How are you?"

She leaned forward and spit in my face. "Baby killer!" she screamed.

I was startled, to say the least. "Baby killer? Baby killer?" I stuttered. People walking through the station stopped and stared.

"Baby killer!" she yelled.

"What are you talking about, lady?" I said. I took my handkerchief out and wiped away the spit. "I just got out of boot camp. I'm in training to repair jet engines. I'm up here visiting my cousin. What are you spittin' on me for?"

"Baby killer!" she screamed again. "Shame on you!" she scolded, her finger in my face. "Shame on you for what you boys are doing over there in Vietnam."

"Lady," I said, "I've never even been to Vietnam, but I want to go. Someone has got to make a down payment on what we have. Our government sent us over there to protect our freedom. We are in Vietnam to make sure that those people enjoy the same liberties that we do."

The old woman was having none of it. "Baby killers," she repeated and then turned and walked away.

My dad was in the Army in World War II. He was a combat engineer. He joined up to operate graders and bulldozers. On the way to Okinawa, the boat he was being transported on was torpedoed and sunk. He was picked up by another boat that was transporting the First Marine Division to the beach. They handed him a rifle. "Congratulations, Mr. George, you're gonna fight with the Marines."

He was in the third wave on Okinawa and was pinned down by enemy fire for five days. He was highly decorated for his actions. I knew that my dad had helped save the world for freedom and that he had done so at great personal cost.

I was never discouraged by that confrontation with the old woman. I knew there was a price to pay for freedom, and her words only served to strengthen my resolve.

When I returned to base, the instructor gathered all of us trainees together in a room. There were sixty young men in my class. "Listen up," he barked. "The two trainees with the highest academic scores on each shift will be allowed to pick their assignment. Gentlemen, six of you can write your own ticket. Six of you will decide where you will spend the remainder of your tour of duty."

Anyone familiar with my high school grade point average of 1.97 would not have given me much of a chance, but again, growing up in an alcoholic environment, you either follow suit or become an overachiever. I had developed a learning technique that has always served me well. I briefly read over the tech manuals and the illustrated parts breakdown. Then, I imagined myself as the fuel molecule or the hydraulic molecule. I visualized myself traveling through the pumps and filters and fluid lines of the component. This technique gave me a depth of understanding that far exceeded anything I would have learned by reading the text and memorizing charts and drawings. It allowed me to comprehend not only how things worked but also why things worked the way they did.

I finished second in my class, and the Air Force was true to their word. "Airman George, where would you like to be stationed?" I thought long and hard on my answer . . . eighteen years old and the world at my fingertips? I selected the United States Air Force Base in Party Town U.S.A, Las Vegas, Nevada.

I was trained to work on the F-111, a fairly new airplane at the time. I also performed maintenance on F-4s, F-105s, and B-52s. It wasn't long before I requested transfer to Guam where my job was to service a fleet of B-52s. The B-52s flew 400 sorties into North Vietnam each day . . . twelve hours round trip. Every second bombing run required a complete change out of all eight fuel and oil filters. I could change oil and fuel filters in my sleep.

Everywhere I went I held down two or more jobs. I would work swing-shift hours at the Air Force Base in Nevada, get off at midnight, eat something, take a shower, and go to bed. At eight in the morning I would head down to Sears and pull a six-hour shift loading trucks, and then it was back to the barracks for a bite to eat and another shift at the airbase . . . seven days a week, week after week. I believed that my accomplishments would surely be the standard by which others would judge me; therefore, I assumed that the more I achieved, the higher my value as a human being. I suppose I still feel that way to a certain extent. I also still believe that we all must pay a price for our freedom. I'm just not sure anymore what that price should be.

23 | The Homecoming

I GOT MY HONORABLE DISCHARGE AND HEADED STRAIGHT FOR home. I ran into Mrs. Donner my first week back. I smiled and called out to her as she approached. A familiar hometown face was exactly what I needed . . . someone from the past to take away the sting of the war. Mrs. Donner had always been kind to me. I used to pack home her groceries from the IGA and took great pride in the fact that I never broke an egg. She had always shown her appreciation for the special attention with a generous tip.

"Mrs. Donner," I said, "how are you? It's really good to see you." She didn't respond. Instead, she glanced about nervously and then turned and crossed to the other side of the street.

"Mrs. Donner," I yelled after her, hurrying to catch up. "It's me, Mrs. Donner . . . Emerson George."

"I know who you are," she said, walking faster. "Leave me alone . . . go away! You shouldn't have come back here to this place. We don't need you here!"

I stopped in my tracks, dumbfounded. What does she mean she doesn't need me here? I ran to catch up and put my hand on her upper arm. She spun around and pushed my hand away.

"Mrs. Donner, it's me, Emerson George. What's wrong?"

She glared back at me. "I know who you are!" she yelled. "You should not have come back here. It's the radicals!" she said, her voice harsh and her eyes filled with fear and hatred. "The tribe has brought in radical Indians from the plains. They are trying to take over Suquamish. You need to leave this place. You don't belong here anymore!" And with that she walked away.

"But I am Indian!" I yelled after her. "I am an Indian!"

She opened her car door and slid inside, closing the door behind her. I shouted out in frustration as her car drove away. "This place is my home!" I yelled, my voice trailing off. "This is where I belong."

I walked up the hill toward home, ignoring the dozen or so people who had stopped to watch the confrontation. Looking up the street I could see the potholes in the road, the uneven sidewalks, and the missing chunk of concrete in front of Mrs. Larkin's old house. I crossed to the other side of the street to avoid it. There were several boys tossing a football by the Congregational Church, and the houses lining the narrow street looked the same as they did before I left. Everything was the same and the lack of change was reassuring. I had a sense of belonging in this place. I walked up to the front gate of Squarehead's house and smiled, knowing that the U.S. Air Force had succeeded in putting some girth on Private George, and the mismatch with Squarehead would now most likely favor the runt.

The old George house stood no worse for wear though everything looked so much smaller. A new family lived there now, but I could see by the broken screen door and the weathered tape covering a crack in the front window that little had changed. I could hear a man's voice inside slurring profanities and a woman's voice screaming back. The door opened and a young Indian boy, maybe six or seven years old, walked outside and sat on the top stair. He looked up at me and I could see he was crying, and I knew there was nothing I could do. I could see the worn spot on the picket fence where the tips of my tennis shoes had dug in a thousand times to propel me up and over. I turned away and walked back down the hill toward my parents' house.

As I got close, I could see that the place was in need of a coat of paint and the grass had gone to seed. I fumbled around in my pocket and found my key, but I knocked to avoid startling anyone. Mom answered the door wearing an old terrycloth robe covered with cigarette burns. The dark circles under her eyes made her look older than her years.

"Emerson," she said, "you are home."

"I'm home, Mom. Is Dad here?"

"Your father went down to the store a few hours ago," she said, turning away. "He said he would be right back. Come in and I will fix you something to eat."

I stepped just inside the door and watched Mom shuffle into the kitchen. "I have some salmon from supper last night," she said. "I can warm that up for you."

I didn't hear her. My eyes went from the fireplace to the table to the pictures on the wall. Everything in the room was familiar. It seemed like I had just left this place . . . this house that I had called home. Everything looked so familiar and yet somehow strangely out of place.

"Emerson," she said, "did you want some of that salmon or not?"

"Salmon? No, thanks, Mom. I'm, ah, not hungry. Look, I'll be back. I'm going to go find Dad."

As I walked out the door, Mom called after me. "Please keep your father out of the tavern, Emerson." I closed the door behind me and stood on the porch for several minutes to catch my breath.

Grandma George's property was about six miles away. I parked on the side of the road by the entrance to Shady Rest. It was a bit of a walk but I was in no great hurry. I found Dad, whiskey bottle in hand, leaning up against a birch tree. He looked old, unshaven . . . his matted hair stuck out from under his cap. I walked up to him from behind, intentionally making noise.

"Dad! It's me, Emerson."

"Son, you are home."

"I am home, Dad."

He shoved the whiskey bottle at me. "You want a pull, son?"

"Not tonight, Dad," I said. "Not tonight."

"Damn cold out here, son! It's always cold out here." He lifted the bottle and took a pull.

"Why don't you come on home with me, Dad. Mom is worried about you."

"No, son. You go back home and visit with your mother. There are things I must do here, and I must stay now and think, and I'll be . . . I'll be along shortly."

"Okay, Dad. I will see you at home. Maybe we can do some fishing in the morning." There was no answer.

I walked slowly back toward my car, and that same helpless feeling that haunted me as a young boy was still there. Even though I knew I was not to blame, I somehow felt guilty for letting my mom down.

Driving back to the house, I thought about Mrs. Donner and what she had said and how she had said it. What could she have possibly meant when she told me that I didn't belong here? I knew it was a time of change in the country, but had things on the reservation changed that much? What did she mean when she said the radicals have been brought into Suquamish? The Civil Rights Movement of the '60s saw protesters from all over the country marching in the South. Blacks had rioted in the inner cities, and people across the country were protesting the war in Vietnam. But there were no marches or riots or protests in Suquamish.

Still, I saw fear and hatred in Mrs. Donner's eyes that day. A kind and gentle lady whom I had known for most of my life was suddenly afraid of me, and I was, at first, at a loss to understand why. It didn't take long for me to realize that things had indeed changed a great deal in the short time I had been away. Tribal folks were gaining strength through the movements of the '60s, and there was a feeling of change in the air. The Suquamish people were no longer satisfied with the status quo. Outsiders had been brought in to administer the services that the Federal Government was mandated to provide via the treaties. The tribe was in a growing phase. They were looking to reclaim lost property and to obtain restitution for promises that were made and never honored. Mrs. Donner and the other non-Indian folks, some of whom held leases on premium tribal waterfront property, could sense the change. The Indians were beginning to rock the boat and it threatened their security, so much so that powerful anti-Indian forces were brought to bear on the Suquamish people. And a silent war would be waged that would force our peaceful coexistence to the breaking point.

24 | The Osterman Chairman

IN 1986, WHEN I APPLIED FOR A FIREWORKS LICENSE, SOMEONE RAISED the issue of where our tax money was going when we paid the tax for our license. How was the tribe using that money? The fireworks' wholesalers elected me their spokesman to bring their voice to the Tribal Council. I did an effective job making recommendations as to where we thought the money should go . . . "self-governance" is what they call it today.

I was gill netting the tribal fishery in Gorst when I was approached about filling the unfinished term of the tribal vice-chairman who never showed up for Tribal Council meetings. I accepted and was appointed vice-chairman and served the one year that was remaining of his term. I was then elected by the General Council to fill that position as vice-chairman and served three years.

The chairman at the time was my first cousin, Georgia George, who is the current treasurer of the Council. As I became more aware and more involved with the operations of tribal government—understanding the dynamics of finance and our own tribal budget, and the dynamics of operating a government—I became disenchanted in the direction our chairman was moving.

It was customary for the Tribal Council Chairman to go back to Congress and testify before a House Subcommittee on Appropriations to specifically discuss Indian issues. We would be given a five-minute slot . . . very strict and formal . . . double-spaced written testimony not to exceed seven pages.

Our chairman and another member of the Council went back there with our prioritized list of needs, and she made a unilateral decision as chairman to create her own list of priorities. She changed the entire testimony, which in my opinion was in direct violation of what her position was. The chairman is a representative, a spokesperson for the tribe . . . someone who would carry our message to Congress.

When I heard she had done that, I decided to run against her for the position of chairman. I told her face to face that I really didn't like the way the leadership was going and that I planned to run against her. With that, she decided not to seek another term as chairman. I was elected by a margin of seventy to eleven to fill the position as chairman. I served my first year as chairman, and I thought I made a positive difference. I changed our course and felt that I had brought some credibility back to the tribe. I was chairman for five years.

An event took place in the mid-1980s on the Port Madison Indian Reservation that, to this day, impacts every tribe on every reservation throughout the entire country. At the time, no one could have possibly foreseen that this one incident would have such dire and far-reaching consequences.

The day had been relatively quiet. It was early evening in the town of Suquamish. At the Tribal Police Station, two officers were sitting at their desks completing what seemed to be an endless pile of bothersome paperwork. The Chief of Police was locked behind the door of his office reading over some reports when the phone rang. The Chief answered. The 911-operator informed him that CenCom had received a complaint from a Suquamish storekeeper. Apparently, there were a couple of men fighting. The Chief hung up and told two of his officers to put out a call for the cruiser to respond and to head downtown to render assistance.

The patrol car arrived first on the scene. The tribal officer found two White males in a pushing and shoving match. He stepped between them, pushed them apart, and told them to break it up. One of the guys backed off. The other fellow, a Mr. Osterman, was loud and belligerent. The officer requested that Mr. Osterman calm down so that everyone could talk about whatever the problem was and clear things up. Mr. Osterman became increasingly belligerent, and when the two other tribal officers arrived on the scene, Mr. Osterman was placed under arrest. They read him his rights, packed him into the patrol car, took him back to the jailhouse, and locked him up.

The two other tribal officers arrived on the scene. Mr. Osterman was subdued, cuffed, and placed under arrest for disturbing the peace and resisting arrest. They read him his rights, packed him into the patrol car, took him back to the jailhouse, and locked him up.

As a consequence of his actions, Mr. Osterman was cited into Suquamish Tribal Court. He hired Mr. Jones, a prominent Poulsbo attorney, to represent him. In Suquamish v. Osterman, the Tribal Court found the accused guilty of disturbing the peace. He was fined the standard amount for the crime and was sentenced to a number of hours of community service. Mr. Jones appealed the case to District Court, claiming that the Suquamish Tribal Police had no jurisdiction over non-Indians in the town of Suquamish within the bounds of the Port Madison Indian Reservation.

I sat for hours with our legal staff and with the other Tribal Council members. We all figured the case was open and shut, and everyone seemed somewhat confused as to the possible motivation for Mr. Jones' filing an appeal on a case where the arrest seemed so obviously righteous.

At the time of the trial, Mr. Jones was living in Suquamish within the bounds of the Port Madison Indian Reservation on roughly forty acres of upland property, land he had leased from the tribe many years earlier. I believe it was around 1970 when he offered to pay the tribe $6,000 a year for twenty-five years. Grandma Martha was co-chairman of the Tribal Council when that lease was signed. She was well aware that sustaining the core of our Tribal Government was an essential part of being recognized for who we were. She knew that to establish and maintain tribal identity that tribal officers must travel to meet influential folks and network with other communities and tribes. She covered the expense of many of these journeys from her own pocket. The Tribal Council decided that this lease money from Mr. Jones would provide a desperately needed source of income.

The lease papers were hastily drawn up—by Mr. Jones of course—and the tribe signed on the dotted line. It was a done deal. The lease did not contain an escalation clause. Six thousand dollars in 1970 was not a bad deal. It was an entire year's salary. In 1990 dollars, however, $6000 was a mere pittance. The lease also provided Mr. Jones with the option of extending the lease at maturity by an additional twenty-five years.

In retrospect, Mr. Jones was a shrewd operator—some say a real shyster—and the tribe got taken to the cleaners though. Without the benefit of hindsight, I believe that the Council felt that they were doing the smart thing. Mr. Jones, however, had his hands on acres of pristine waterfront reservation property, and the lease allowed him the freedom to use the land as he saw fit. He immediately sub-divided, put up houses, and subleased eighty-five waterfront lots to upper-middle-class Whites.

I knew that the original twenty-five-year lease was coming to an end and that Mr. Jones was still paying only $6,000 a year while making a small fortune on his investment. Could it be that Mr. Jones saw the Osterman trial as an opportunity to undermine tribal authority to the point of assimilation or even abrogating the treaty?

I was also aware of the fact that Mr. Jones had an intense hatred for Indians since I had experienced his bigotry and prejudice first hand. My wife Sue and I were having dinner one night at Mitzel's restaurant in Poulsbo. Mr. Jones and his wife came into the restaurant with another man. The waitress seated them at the table next to us. Sue was sitting back-to-back to Mrs. Jones, and I was sitting with my back to the wall, eye-to-eye with Mr. Jones. He caught my eye and then turned to the other fellow at his table and said, more than loud enough to be heard, "Hitler had the right idea. He should have eliminated all minorities."

The Osterman case came before the District Court, and the Court ruled in the tribe's favor. Mr. Jones appealed the case to Federal Court. The Federal Court ruled in the tribe's favor. Mr. Jones appealed again, and the Appellate Court upheld the District Court's finding. Strangely, Mr. Jones did not seem discouraged by his courtroom losses. I took note of the fact that he actually seemed smug, as if he had a master plan, understandable considering his recent references to the Fuehrer.

Mr. Jones had somehow managed to get the Osterman case on the docket of the United States Supreme Court. I strongly suspect that he had help greasing the skids, like maybe from an anti-Indian, influential, perennial senator from his home state.

The highest court in the land ruled that Tribal Police acted unlawfully when they arrested Mr. Osterman for disturbing the peace in the town of Suquamish. They overturned the decision of the lower courts. Mr. Osterman was cleared of the charges against him. He would pay neither penalty nor penance for his errant behavior. The Supreme Court decision meant, quite literally, that the Suquamish

Tribal Police, and for that matter all tribal police on all Indian reservations in the United States, no longer had jurisdiction over non-Indians breaking the law within the bounds of their reservations.

As I traveled about the country, conducting tribal business, I was introduced to national Indian leaders as the Tribal Chairman of the Suquamish. They referred to me as the *Osterman Chairman*. And though there was no intended disrespect, there was also no shortage of free advice regarding the importance of carefully selecting one's battles.

The High Court reversal had an immediate impact in every state where there are indigenous peoples. The ruling created a jurisdictional dispute that resulted in virtual lawlessness. What followed would shake the very foundation of tribal government.

25 | A Decade of Decadence

IT DIDN'T TAKE LONG FOR DRUG DEALERS, CON MEN, RABBLE-ROUSERS, and every other kind of unimaginable, lowlife scum to move into the Promised Land. The Port Madison Indian Reservation, along with reservations across the entire country, became jurisdictional gray areas. Methamphetamine labs popped up everywhere. Crack cocaine dealers found that they could ply their trade with virtual impunity, and the beauty of it was that the majority of their young clientele already had one foot firmly implanted in dysfunction, and there was little, or nothing, that tribal enforcement could do about it.

As I left the house one morning, Sue yelled after me to pick up the day's mail. The post office was on the way into town, so I pulled in, parked, entered, and opened our box. There was a postcard from our daughter who was off at college. I turned the postcard over and smiled. She wrote that she was doing well with her studies, missed her mom and dad, and expected to drop by the house the next weekend. There were several magazines, a credit card application, and a hand-addressed envelope from an old acquaintance of mine, now a deputy with the Sheriff's Department. I remember thinking it a bit strange that I would get a letter from this guy. I was in a hurry to get downtown, so I stuck the envelope in my shirt pocket, hopped in the truck, and left.

I drove down to the Tribal Police Station and parked out front. I entered the building and knocked on the Chief's office door. The Chief and I had a great deal of respect for each and, when he saw who it was, he got up from his chair and opened the door, extending his hand. We shook, and he invited me into his office. He asked me to please have a seat and motioned to one of several chairs that surrounded his desk. I scooted my chair closer to his desk and he returned to his chair and sat down.

"How have you been Emerson?"

"I have been fine, very busy. Things are as good as can be expected under the circumstances."

The Chief opened his top desk drawer and offered me a cigar. I'm never one to turn down a man's hospitality. He clipped the ends, handed me the cigar, and pulled a flip-top lighter from his pocket. We both took a minute to savor the taste. I blew a stream of smoke upward. "Very good," I said. "Thank you."

The Chief leaned back in his chair and exhaled a smoke ring that drifted up and dissipated. "What is it that I can do for you?" he said.

I sat forward on the edge of the chair. I told him that I wanted him to call ahead to the Poulsbo Police Department and give them a description of my truck. I had a brand new, four-door, Chevy Crew Cab at the time.

"Why would I want to do that?" he said.

"Tell them that a Chevy Crew Cab, four-door, pickup truck just drove through the reservation at high rates of speed."

The Chief was confused. "I suppose I can do that," he said, "but what's the point?"

"The point is," I said, "I'm going to drive through the 35-mile-per-hour zone in Poulsbo doing 37 mph and see if they pull me over and give me a ticket."

The Chief leaned forward and smiled. "You're gonna test them?"

"Yes," I nodded, "test them. I'm going to challenge the Osterman ruling using Poulsbo's Civil Code. When they arrest me for speeding, I will be cited into Municipal Court, and I will argue that, since I don't elect Poulsbo city officials, their police force should have no jurisdiction over me."

The Chief leaned back and kicked his feet up on the desktop, folded his hands behind his head and stared at the ceiling as if admiring the view. Another smoke ring swirled upward. "Interesting plan," he said, "but why the Poulsbo Police? Why not the Sheriff's Department or the State Patrol?"

"Because," I said, "we elect county officials and state officials, but we don't elect the officials of a municipality. What I want to do is create the lawlessness over a municipality very similar to what they have done over the Indian reservation. You know when you go to Canada you don't elect Canadian officials, and yet you still must abide by their laws. To me it's the same situation."

The Chief walked around the corner of his desk and stood in front of me, eye to eye. "Emerson," he said, "I like the way you think, but it won't get you what you want. They will arrest you and fine you, and the only thing you're gonna get out of the whole deal is a hefty fine and a big hike in your car insurance." He walked past me toward the coffeepot. "Let me tell you what happened yesterday," he said as he poured sugar in his cup. "One of my officers pulled over this White guy. He was speeding . . . crossing the centerline from fog line to fog line. One of his taillights was burnt out; his license tabs were expired. Would you like a cup of coffee?"

"Coffee? Yes," I said, "black, please . . . no sugar." He filled two Styrofoam cups, handed one to me, and then walked to his chair and sat down.

"So, anyway," he continued, "this guy rolls his window down and the vehicle smells like a whiskey gin. When my officer asked this fella if he knew why he had been pulled over, the guy slurred an entire sentence into one word. He produced a driver's license that belonged to his father. It had a hole punched in it. He couldn't present proof of insurance, had no registration, no seat belt, faulty equipment, you name it."

"So," I said, "the officer arrested the guy, right?"

"No, we didn't bring him in. My officer called the Kitsap County Sheriff, and when the deputy showed up he let the drunk go. The deputy told my officer that he had made an illegal stop because he had no jurisdiction. I swear to God he let the drunken idiot go. I'm just sick about it. I'm surprised the guy didn't end up killing somebody on his way home."

My jaw tightened and my blood burned. "What I'm hearing," I said, "is if someone gets stopped on the Port Madison Indian Reservation by one of our Tribal Police officers, and the officer determines that the driver is a non-Indian, then our guy has got to let the driver go? That's it?"

"That's it," said the Chief, shaking his head. "That's the ugly truth of it."

I was livid . . . my voice became progressively louder as I spouted a rush of rhetorical questions. "So what does that do to the non-Indians on the reservation? What happens when someone in that inebriated state can traverse the city with virtual impunity? What happens if one of the folks downtown has an aid call?

What if one of your officers is being shot at? What are you going to do?"

The Chief ground out his cigar in the ashtray. "I've spent the better part of the morning in my office," he said, "asking myself those very same questions. We're going to respond to the situation, of course, even though we have no jurisdiction over non-Indians on the reservation. We'll just hope for the best, you know? We'll just hope for the best."

I stood up, walked over to the window, and took a deep breath, slowly exhaling, trying to calm myself. I gazed out at the houses and the Indian children playing in the street. My heart was pounding in my chest. I couldn't think. Then I remembered the envelope in my pocket. I removed it and slid my finger into the seal. Inside was a handwritten note that indicated the Kitsap County Sheriff had instructed his deputies to not respond or assist tribal police.

I read the memo out loud. The Chief got out of his chair and walked over to me. He took the memo and read it to himself. "County has been instructed to not show up?" he said.

I nodded. I had no energy left for anger. "So, Chief," I said, "as tax paying citizens living on fee property within the bounds of the Port Madison Indian Reservation, our non-Indian folks also have a legitimate complaint. I mean, if there is a domestic dispute . . ."

The Chief interrupted, "Then my guys can just break it up and hope it works out, knowing that County will not respond. We're not going to just sit there and do nothing."

"My friend," I said, "the County has been directed not to respond to tribal requests for assistance. That's anarchy, Chief. Lawlessness and anarchy."

As the decade progressed, it became more and more evident that there was a concerted political effort to rein the natives in. There was collusion between local government officials, and bigotry was the weapon of choice. The directive to not respond to aid calls apparently came from the office of the County Prosecutor. It was reported to me by Indians and non-Indians alike that whenever 911 calls were received from a 598 Suquamish telephone prefix that the 911 operator would ask the callers if they were Indian or non-Indian. The answer would determine whether or not emergency services were dispatched. This went on for close to ten years. To the Suquamish people, this bigotry was no different than Black and White bathrooms, segregated restaurants, or being relegated to riding in the back of the bus.

I contacted County officials to complain about their prejudicial policies. I pleaded our case at every level. The issue of County not responding was not just one of jurisdiction. Property, life, and limb were being placed in jeopardy. Aid calls went unanswered. Ambulances were often not dispatched. Requests for assistance by Tribal Police officers were ignored. Drug trafficking went unchecked. The drug trade was poisoning our tribal youth and tearing the Suquamish people apart. It reached a point where fire departments refused to respond to structural fires on the reservation. They claimed that since the Suquamish tribe didn't pay property taxes, there was no money appropriated to pay for their services; the truth was quite the opposite.

I was living in a 1,400 square foot, street blockhouse in Suquamish at the time. I paid about $1,200 a year in property taxes, and there were sixteen houses on my street alone. That's close to $19,000 in property taxes, just from my street, that went directly into County coffers. The County Commissioner knew that every house that was built added around $1,000 in taxes to the base revenue, so they divided Suquamish into 25-foot lots, and $1,000 in property taxes per house was filtered through the County Auditor via the taxing process.

The way I saw it the County collected these property taxes from the residents of the Port Madison Indian Reservation, and yet they provided no services. They didn't provide law enforcement, emergency aid, or fire fighting. We paid our own power, sewer, and water, plus our property taxes on top of that. I argued that this practice was tantamount to taxation without representation, the very foundation of the American Revolution. I felt like I was talking to the wall.

I attempted to take the battle to the print media only to find that the primary area newspaper was polarized against the concerns of the Suquamish Tribe. Instead of acting as a neutral medium for a wide range of community viewpoints, the newspaper chose instead to take every opportunity to add fuel to the fire. My interviews were twisted and manipulated to omit key comments. I was repetitively misquoted or, under the guise of poetic license, my words were changed or rearranged to alter the very meaning of my message. I had hoped to use the press to overcome fear and ignorance and build community understanding. Instead, I was skillfully portrayed as an individual full of prejudice and hatred. There is a fine line between freedom fighter and terrorist, and I learned a valuable lesson. I learned that the power of the pen could easily tip the scale of justice.

I met with the Editorial Board of the newspaper and pleaded with them to at least have the common decency to give the people of the Suquamish Tribe an opportunity to respond to what I considered some of the hate literature that was coming out in their paper. My request was refused. Instead, the public was bombarded with a weekly barrage of negative editorials written by a tenured female reporter whose words painted all Indians as drunken, self-serving, dysfunctional troublemakers.

In the mid-'80s, there was a cross burning in front of the house of a mixed family within the bounds of the reservation. Two Whites had adopted two Black kids, and someone burned a cross in their yard. The County Prosecutor did nothing. He had a standing policy of refusing to prosecute non-Indian offenders on the reservation, but if a tribal member got busted in Poulsbo, he would go after them with a vengeance.

The Tribal Police Chief had to contact the FBI in order to get help for this resident of the Port Madison Indian Reservation. The FBI came on to the reservation to investigate a legitimate hate crime. The perpetrators were apprehended. They were turned over to County because they were underage high school students. These *kids* ended up with community service. I was left to wonder how much community service one might get for burning a cross in Alabama?

In the early '90s, Steve Boyer, a retired State Patrol officer, ran for Kitsap County Sheriff. I asked Mr. Boyer point blank how he perceived the Suquamish Police Department as compared to the State Patrol or the County Sheriff, or Poulsbo or Bainbridge Island police officers." He said that the only difference he saw was the color of the uniform.

Mr. Boyer, along with the new County Prosecutor, worked hand in hand with the tribe to eliminate many of these barriers. There is now an agreement with the County Sheriff where, if Tribal Officers pull over a non-Indian driving on the reservation, the offender can be cited into Tribal Court. The 911 operators no longer ask for tribal affiliation. They just dispatch. The situation is improving, but for one nightmarish decade, we fought for our autonomy against every attempt at subjugation and assimilation while the very future of our people hung in the balance. The tribe continues to gnaw away at these prejudices and to work very hard to gain respect. Unfortunately, the racism and prejudice that blocks our progress at nearly every turn in the road also emanates from within and eats away like a cancer at the very soul of our people.

26 | Insurrection

THE TRIBAL COUNCIL IS THE HEART OF INDIAN GOVERNMENT. THE elected members of the Council discuss and vote on issues that impact the lives and well being of every Indian on the reservation. The Tribal Council Constitution and By-laws were specifically written to allow only Suquamish tribal members to speak at General Council meetings. These meetings, as a rule, are held annually on the third Sunday of March. I knew that my people were faced with serious issues that required timely solutions, so I opted for a second General Council meeting in September. It was at that September meeting that the Suquamish community would bear witness to a complete insurrection of our Tribal Police Department based not on fact but entirely on the ugly specter of racism.

The afternoon of the General Council meeting, Tribal Police received a phone call. The call came from the low-income-housing area on the reservation. A resident was complaining about a neighbor who, apparently, was harassing them in violation of a restraining order. The perpetrator, a fellow named Billy Walks Backwards, had a rap sheet as long as your arm.

Tribal Police and Billy Walks Backwards were well acquainted with each other, and a trip to Billy's house in response to some citizen's complaint was a routine occurrence. Billy was an Indian, but not Suquamish. He had married a Suquamish Indian woman. It was difficult to find anyone who, at some time or another, hadn't had some difficulty with Billy Walks Backwards. He carried a chip on his shoulder a city block long, and he left a trail of bad blood wherever he went. When Billy was sober and on his best behavior, he was disrespectful and spiteful. When Billy was drinking, he was volatile and unpredictable.

The low-income-housing area where Billy lived consisted of row after row of small one- and two-bedroom dwellings with little space between them for privacy. The neighbors who lived on either side of Billy were so fond of his demonstrated skill at the art of interpersonal relations that both families found it necessary to obtain restraining orders. Apparently, when Billy was inebriated, he was unable to contain his impulses, and he would often share his warm, personable self with his neighbors . . . usually at the most inopportune times.

After receiving the harassment call, Tribal Officers drove down to the housing project. The patrol car pulled up onto the curb and parked. The police sergeant and another officer walked through Billy's yard and up onto his porch. The sergeant knocked on the door. "Billy! This is the Tribal Police. We have a complaint from your neighbor that you have violated the restraining order. Please open the door." The officers could hear pots and pans banging around inside. They again rapped on the door. "Billy! Billy Walks Backwards! This is the Tribal Police. We have a . . . "

The door opened and Billy staggered onto the porch. He had a fifth of whiskey in his hand, and he was slobbering drunk. "What the hell do you assholes want?"

The police sergeant stepped forward within inches of Billy's chest. Billy backed up against the doorframe.

"Watch your tongue, Billy. Your neighbors have lodged a complaint against you for violating a restraining order."

Billy took a big swig from the bottle. A stream of whiskey trickled down his chin and dripped onto his filthy tee shirt. "Screw them asshole sons-a-bitches," he growled, spewing booze on the sergeant's uniform.

The sergeant was in no mood for one of Billy's tirades. He had taken his verbal abuse more times than he cared to remember. "Billy," he said, "the law says we have to give you a warning so consider this your warning, and I swear to God if you so much as look crooked at your neighbor I'll be back down here so fast it'll make your head spin. Do you have a problem understanding any of what I've just said?"

Billy stumbled back inside the house and slammed the door, uttering a string of colorful metaphors.

The sergeant raised his voice, "I'm not gonna mess with you on this, Billy. I suggest that you find something to do that will keep you out of trouble unless you want to spend the rest of the night behind bars." The officers stepped down from the porch and walked over to the neighbor who had called in the complaint. The sergeant knocked on the door, and a woman answered, "Good evening," he said. "We just wanted to let you know that we've had a talk with Billy, and we don't expect you to have any more problems with him tonight. If he bothers you folks again, just give us a call."

Minutes after arriving back at the station another call came in. Billy was again harassing his neighbor. The sergeant shook his head. "Damn that guy! There's no way he's gonna make this easy. I don't expect him to go along peacefully. Let's roll two units."

My son Brian was a cadet with the Suquamish Police Department, and he had completed extensive cadet training. He was an Explorer Scout for the Bainbridge Island Police Department and would later graduate from the Academy, scoring at the top of his class in driving and marksmanship. Brian was pretty well plugged into the Tribal Police Department at the time, so when the second call came in, Brian went along in the patrol car to assist.

When they got to Billy's house, the front door was open. Brian, the sergeant, and two officers walked up the stairs and onto the porch. The sergeant stood in the doorway facing Billy, who was standing several feet inside the house. "Billy Walks Backwards, I warned you that if we had to come down here again we were gonna haul you in. Step outside, please." Billy spewed a string of profanities.

As the four officers entered the house, Billy assumed a defensive stance. The sergeant pulled out his mace and sprayed Billy right in the face, whereupon Billy got violently pissed. He began kicking, screaming, and swinging his arms like a wild man. Two of the officers tackled him in the living room, and the tangle of bodies fell over an end table, knocked over a floor lamp, and landed in a clump on the floor. It took all four of them to hold him down and cuff him. The sergeant read Billy his rights. Billy was placed in a patrol car, spitting and cussing up a storm. He spent the entire trip to the jailhouse cussing and banging his head against the patrol car window. They carried him inside the jailhouse and the sergeant locked him up.

There was only one minor problem. The officers, thinking that they had done everything by the book, discovered that the second phone call was from the neighbor that lived on the other side of Billy's house. In other words, they had responded to a complaint from the first neighbor and gave Billy the prerequisite warning.

They then arrested him on a complaint from a different neighbor. Unfortunately, the law states that both complaints must come from the same person and, therefore, the arrest was deemed illegal. They had sprayed, tackled, and arrested Billy Walks Backwards, and now they had to let him go.

Billy traversed the entire length of town telling everyone who would listen that a bunch of White police officers had roughed him up and illegally hauled him to jail. He told the entire town that the arrest was a conspiracy . . . that I had my son on the Police Department and that the White officers on the force were all a bunch of thugs doing whatever I told them to do! "The White Gestapo" he hollered, "busted into my house and beat me up for nothing."

There were numerous bruises as well as a convincing stream of dried blood on the side of Billy's face from where he had pummeled himself against the patrol-car window. "I wasn't doin' nothin," he screamed. "They just came into my house and busted the place up and beat me up. They do whatever George tells 'em to do, and I for one ain't gonna tolerate this shit!"

Unfortunately, racism and hatred are human characteristics, and Billy Walks Backwards attracted quite a following of angry Indians. There were many in the community who were already outwardly suspicious of anyone White, let alone a White man packing a gun and wearing a badge on their reservation. Billy ended up at the Suquamish Tavern where a room full of inebriated Indians made an ideal audience for his claims of injustice and plans for retribution. It didn't take more than a drink or two for many of these folks to enthusiastically rally to his side yelling, "Emerson George and his White thugs!"

He yelled, "Are we gonna tolerate it?"

A resounding "No!" went up from the crowd. The hook was set.

"Tonight I'm gonna show up at that Council meeting and blast that son of a bitch! Are you with me?"

"Yeah!" came the outcry. "Let's get rid of them White pigs!"

My cousin, Chuck, who had stopped by the tavern after work, finished his beer, deposited several dollars on the bar, and quietly slipped out the back door.

Back at the police station, the Chief had gathered his people around him. "Listen up, fellas, I'm getting reports that we have a lot of folks in the community worked up over this thing. Brian, go and give your dad a call and tell him I want to see him before he goes to the Council meeting." Brian nodded.

"Lieutenant, take a couple of men over to the tavern and stake the place out. Let me know if anything gets out of hand. The rest of you get out in the community and be on your toes. I don't want anyone getting hurt tonight. Do you all understand?" Everyone nodded.

As Chuck pulled into my driveway, I was just getting into my car. He parked alongside me and rolled down his window. "Hey, we need to talk," he said. "Where are you headed?"

I was bent over in my car placing a pile of papers on the front seat. "There's a Tribal Council meeting tonight," I said over my shoulder. As I turned, I could see that Chuck was upset. "Is everything okay, Chuck?" I asked. "You look like you've just seen a ghost."

"It's Billy Walks Backwards, man. He's down at the tavern and he's got a bunch a' folks all worked up. He's drinking and bragging about showing up at the meeting tonight and getting a piece of you. You gotta stay home tonight. It's not safe for you down there."

"Thanks, Chuck," I said. "Thanks for letting me know."

The front door opened and Sue walked out on the porch. "Brian just called," she said. "The Chief wants you to stop by and see him on your way to the meeting. Brian sounded upset. Is something wrong? What's wrong? Chuck, what's wrong?"

Chuck turned back to me. "The guy is gunning for you. I'm telling you, that guy is nuts and he's gunning for you."

I put my hand on Chuck's shoulder. "I hear you, okay, but I have to be there."

Chuck took a slow, deep breath, sighed, and shook his head. "Be careful, okay?" Nodding to Sue, he got back in his car and stuck his head out the window. "Listen up, man, I'll be there tonight. I'll be like a fly on the wall. If that guy makes a move for you, I'm all over him. You know what I mean? I'll be all over him."

"Thanks, Chuck, thanks."

Billy Walks Backwards didn't worry me nearly as much as facing my wife. When I turned back to say goodbye, I could see she wasn't too happy. "I'll see you tonight. Okay?" I said. "Don't worry about what Chuck said. He's had a few beers. Everything will be just fine. I'll see you tonight after the meeting."

Sue took several steps forward and crossed her arms. She wasn't buying any of it. "What are you doing?" she said. "Why do you feel like you have to be the one to risk everything?"

"I have no choice, okay? It's my responsibility."

She walked to the edge of the porch and glared down at me, her hands on her hips. "Why is it always you who has to be responsible? What makes you the one?"

I slid into the seat of the car and Sue raised her voice. "I can't believe that you're willing to risk everything because you feel obligated! Obligated to whom? These people don't care if you feel obligated! What about us . . . our family? You don't owe these people anything. You don't have to go down there tonight. Just stay home. Please, just stay home and wait until things calm down."

"I love you," I said. "I gotta to go. Everything will be fine. I'll see you when I get home." I started the car, backed up and headed up the driveway. I looked in the rear view mirror, and I could see her standing on the porch screaming after me, but I couldn't hear her.

When I arrived at the station, the Chief met me at the door. "Emerson," he said, "I'm glad you got the message."

We shook hands. "What's up, Chief?"

"Come in, come in," he said. "Listen, I'm really concerned about your safety at the meeting tonight. I think there may be some trouble."

"Yes, I know," I said. "My cousin Chuck came by the house a little while ago and told me that things were getting a little out of hand down at the tavern. He said I should stay home, but you know I can't. I've gotta tell you, Chief, I'm a bit worried. I'm hearing that Billy's got a lot of folks pissed off."

The Chief turned and walked into the back room. "Come with me," he said. He removed a set of keys from his pocket and opened a cabinet door. "I want you to wear this tonight," he said. He pulled out a garment and held it up.

"A bulletproof vest?"

"A bulletproof vest," he said. "Kevlar . . . good stuff . . . lightweight. You won't even be able to tell you're wearing anything. Try it on."

I took the vest and studied it for several seconds. "Under my shirt?" I said. The Chief nodded. I took off my shirt and pulled on the vest. He said it made me look bigger. I'm thinking that's a good thing and I thanked him.

As I turned and walked toward the front door, he yelled after me. "I'll be there," he said. "I will be at the meeting tonight, and I will sit with you, and everything will be okay."

Billy Walks Backwards showed up at the Council meeting as expected. He had his entire inebriated support group in tow. Everybody at the meeting had heard Billy's story. His followers were in the minority, but there was a steady, low rumble of angry voices. The stage was set. Billy Walks Backwards had a bone to pick. I pounded my gavel several times to call the meeting to order. Billy Walks Backwards immediately thrust his fist into the air.

I cleared my throat. "The Chair recognizes Mr. Billy Walks Backwards."

Billy jumped to his feet and pointed his finger at me. His face was flush with anger. "I wanna talk about you, Emerson George, Mr. High and Mighty!" he screamed. "I wanna talk to you about your White Gestapo and your . . ."

One of the Tribal Council members stood up. "Point of order, Mr. Chairman!" he yelled. "Point of order!

This man is not a tribal member! He is not allowed to speak at this meeting!"

Billy glared back at him, and a rumble of protest arose from the crowd.

Now, as Tribal Council Chairman, it was not uncommon for me to bend the rules and ask for input from non-Indian community members, knowing that when the Council was hard-pressed to make a decision, they stood to benefit from hearing a variety of viewpoints but, in this particular situation, I figured it would be a good time to stand on policy. I slammed the gavel several times and again the room fell quiet. I apologized to Billy and explained to him that our Constitution and By-laws specifically forbade him to speak. I told him that if he wanted to speak to me after the meeting that I would be more than happy to listen to his concerns.

His eyes narrowed in a cold stare. Several people called out to let Billy speak his piece.

I rapped the gavel twice. "Because he is a non-tribal member," I repeated, "I cannot allow Billy Walks Backwards to speak. I'm sorry, but those are the by-laws of our constitution. Billy, please be seated."

You could hear a pin drop in the room. All eyes were on him, waiting for his next move. We stared at each other in silence for what seemed an eternity. My jaw was set, and Billy stood with his fists clenched and his eyes fixed.

Chuck had been standing on one side up against the wall, and I watched him slip through the crowd until he was standing right behind Billy. He figured that all hell was about to break loose, and he wanted the first shot at Billy. The Chief tensed and sat forward in his chair. I knew that there would be no room for further amenities.

"Be seated, NOW!" I said.

Billy looked at the Chief and studied the faces of the people around him. Many of them, I'm sure, had first-hand experiences with Billy's errant behavior. He looked back at me, muttered something under his breath, and slowly sat down.

There was still a scattering of tribal members in the crowd that were more than willing to speak out against the Police Department. Several hands went up. I pointed to an old friend of mine in the back of the room. "The Chair recognizes Mr. Ron Purser." I had known Ron since we were boys. We hunted and fished together. I helped him build a woodshed in his backyard. My kids played with his kids. "Ron," I said, "you have the floor."

Ron stared at the ground and spoke, at first barely loud enough to be heard. "Our Police Chief is a White man."

Shouts of protest came from the crowd, and I rapped the gavel.

"I will have order in this Council meeting," I yelled. "Ron has the floor." I asked Ron to continue.

Billy Walks Backwards was unable to contain himself. He jumped to his feet shouting, "Purser said your Gestapo Police Chief is a White man!" The crowd exploded in anger. Several men stood and their fists pounded the air. The Chief stood behind me and scanned the room.

I again rapped the gavel. "Order! Order!" The place got quiet. I pointed the business end of the gavel at Billy.

"Billy Walks Backwards!" I said, "I will not tell you again! Another interruption and I will have you forcefully removed from these chambers." He sat down, and several in the crowd shouted racist slurs. My threat to forcefully eject Billy from the Council meeting for disruptive and disrespectful behavior was, of course, interpreted by Billy's followers as vindication of his story.

I asked Ron if he had anything more to say. He cleared his throat. "Our Police Chief is a White man," he mumbled. "How can he understand our reservation life?"

I spun around in my chair and pointed at the Chief.

"This White man here?" I yelled above the noise. "You ask how this White man can understand reservation life?" The place quieted down. I turned to the Chief and apologized. I told him that I had to break a promise I had made to him that I would never bring up his family life. He nodded and I could tell that he understood.

"This man," I said, "is married to the vice-chairman of the Squaxin Island Tribe. He was a police officer in their Police Department. His son is a registered and enrolled Squaxin Island tribal member. You accuse this man of not understanding the Indian way of life when his wife and his children are Indian?"

The rumble from the crowd only got louder. They didn't hear a word I said. It was clear to me that there was nothing more to say . . . this scattering of folks, maybe twenty percent of those in attendance, came to the Council meeting that night in support of Billy Walks Backwards, and when my words and actions failed to validate their prejudices, they could no longer hear my voice. They saw a bigoted, non-Indian police chief, a bigoted lieutenant and an Aryan Nations sergeant. They did not have the facts. I tried to provide them with the facts, but they chose to close their ears to the truth.

A petition was brought forward demanding the Chief's resignation. The sergeant and lieutenant were also asked to resign. The lieutenant wasn't even a White man. He was a Ute Indian from Utah. He and his sister were adopted and raised in a non-Indian home, but they were both enrolled.

The next day the Chief resigned and the lieutenant and sergeant followed suit. I don't blame them. The price was too high. No reason for them to hang around and listen to their department being raked over the coals when there were jobs available in White communities that paid better and offered more benefits. Jobs free from rampant alcohol and drug addiction, free from prejudice and hatred, and free from confusing issues of jurisdiction.

The insurrection of the Police Department did not sit well with me. It was an inexcusable miscarriage of justice, instigated by drunken rabble-rousers. I knew the Chief and his officers to be men of courage and integrity. I knew that our Police Department was Black and White . . . you break the law, you pay the price. Everywhere on the reservation I see powerful evil spirits of racism, hatred, and bigotry. Drugs and alcohol continue to cause irreparable damage. When I walk among my people today, I see hatred and anger in their faces and as always, it will be the children, the innocent ones, who will pay an all-too-familiar price.

27 | Trail of Terror

THE DAY AFTER THE MEETING, BILLY WALKS BACKWARDS FILED A lawsuit accusing me, the members of the Tribal Council, and the Police Department of violating an Indian's civil rights. I spent four hours in deposition in Seattle sitting directly across the table from Billy and his attorney.

That evening I was scheduled to dedicate a daycare center in the low-income-housing area where Billy Walks Backwards lived with his wife. As we walked by his house, Billy was standing out on his porch with several of his supporters. I could see the hatred in his eyes. That night when Sue and I got home there was a phone message on the answering machine. The message was from Billy. I clearly recognized his voice. Billy had left a very explicit message for me. "I'm gonna rape your wife. I'm gonna rape your daughter, and I'll probably have my way with your son while I've got you hog-tied. I might even drag your mother in on this."

Sue was in tears. I saved the message and called the Police Department. Unfortunately, before I could dial *69 and trace the call, another phone call eliminated the opportunity.

To a small group of his misguided followers, Billy Walks Backwards had become a martyr, a defender of the under-privileged. To me, and my family, Billy Walks Backwards was a nightmare . . . disturbed and twisted. As the legal battle escalated, so did the harassment. Soon, hate mail started showing up in our mailbox. The letters were coming almost daily. I tried to catch them in the mail before Sue saw them so she wouldn't be upset. I turned all of those letters over to the tribal legal staff. In March of 1999, I was in Pearl Harbor on business when several hate letters showed up in the mail. Sue opened them. To say the letters frightened her would be a gross understatement.

She called me and was extremely upset. I flew home immediately. I tried, and failed, to get a restraining order through the tribal court system. They wouldn't issue a restraining order because they were afraid of this guy. Sue ended up going to the County and getting a County restraining order. I could handle the personal threats, but when Billy threatened my wife and children, he crossed the line. I would not tolerate his cowardice.

In our culture, when an Indian is considered of lesser character, they can be excluded or banished from the community. Banishment is a way of life in tribal communities, and banishment is still on the books as a tribal law that can be enforced. I started the process to banish Billy from the reservation. The numerous hate letters were more than sufficient documentation. Billy knew that banishment was inevitable, so he volunteered to banish himself. His banishment was twisted around to the point where word in the community was that I had unjustly arranged to banish Billy from his home on the reservation where his wife and children lived.

Our lead attorney was representing Tribal Council as well as those tribal employees who were named in the suit. The Police Department had no faith in our legal staff, and I guess, under the circumstances, I didn't blame them. They hired two of their own attorneys to represent the four of them. Since it was a Federal case, the U.S. Attorney General sent legal representation to assist. There were three of those government attorneys. Billy Walks Backwards had one attorney.

Before the case ever went to court, my attorney called me in and told me that he had met with Billy's attorney and the two of them had agreed to settle out of court. He told me that we were going to give Billy Walks Backwards $10,000. I was extremely upset. "You have got to be shitting me!" I yelled. "This man threatened my family. This man threatened me. This man caused an insurrection of our Police Department. Why in the hell would you settle with this man?" After I stopped fuming, I got my answer. As soon as we settled with Billy for the $10,000, they would send him a bill for $63,000 in attorney's fees because Billy's case was deemed to be frivolous. Billy's attorney, who had taken the case *pro bono*, hire for fee, would take his cut out of the $10,000 settlement.

My family and I lived with that nightmare for two years, from the beginning of 1997 through the end of 1998. Billy Walks Backwards still lives in the area and, by his very nature, is a threat to the welfare of my family. But Billy is a tangible nemesis, a man who telegraphs his anger and his intentions. He is a sorry human being who finds his courage in a bottle and claims victory in the threats he makes against women and children. I can see into this man . . . the wickedness in his heart and the evil of his spirit. If need be, I am ready and able to deal with his cowardice. However, I was not prepared to deal with the betrayal and deception that awaited me in Council chambers, not from rabble-rousers or disgruntled supporters of Billy Walks Backwards but from tribal leaders—men who I feel betrayed their position of authority—men who, under the guise of the governing body of the Suquamish Tribe, made choices that would ultimately affect every tribal member . . . choices that were not in the best interest of our people . . . choices that only served to satisfy the hidden, self-serving agendas of a select few.

 **28 | Casino**

I WAS COUNCIL CHAIRMAN WHEN THE TRIBE ENTERED INTO CLASS 3 Gaming negotiations with the State of Washington. When the state originally offered gaming to the Indians, the proposed guidelines and controls were very restrictive. The Suquamish Tribal negotiators were very positive and proactive in support of Indian gaming and were instrumental in convincing government officials to increase the allowable size and scope of our casino. With approval from the State in hand, we went looking for funding.

I remember several of us catching the "Redeye" to Wisconsin on a Sunday night in December. We planned to meet with the Winnebago Tribal Council to talk about the possibility of their tribe's loaning us money to build our casino. Our original itinerary was to fly into Chicago and then on to St. Paul, Wisconsin. Someone from their tribe was scheduled to meet us in St. Paul and drive us out to their Tribal Council meeting where we would lay out our prospectus and our business plan.

We arrived in Chicago on schedule at around 6:00 in the morning. While we were waiting for a flight to St. Paul, a blizzard hit the Chicago area with a vengence. All outgoing flights were cancelled, traffic was snarled, nothing was moving. I ended up spending three days in my suit at O'Hare International. When the weather finally cleared, we flew home. We never got to visit the Winnebago Reservation. Their representatives did end up flying out here to look at our site and check out our business plan and our proposed structure. There was a great deal of interest on their part, but the deal fell through when, in the middle of negotiations, they had an insurrection of their Tribal Council.

With that avenue gone, we entertained numerous proposals from management firms. They all offered to fund and manage the casino. They would build the hotel, bring in their own staff, from bartenders to dealers, and pay off the loan. In exchange for their services, they would take a healthy percentage of the gross.

Indian gaming was a new market at the time. There was no shortage of horror stories about Indian casinos operating in the red and going under, unable to pay the management contract. After exploring those options and completing our market study, we decided to seek private finacing and run the casino ourselves. We hired our own staff. We were the first tribe in the state, if not the nation, to open and operate a casino without bringing in a management company. If we failed, it would be because of our own ineptness, not because of some outside entity.

We hired a consultant to help us create the infrastucture. Another consultant was hired to help us build the facility. We approached several banks with our proposal. We finally found a lending institution in Utah that agreed to finance the project. We bought the tables, selected the chips, and did everything that management companies had done for other tribes.

As a condition of opening our casino, the State of Washington required that we notify the local fire department, law enforcement agencies, and elected county officials. That was a requirement for all Indian gaming in the state. The intent was to free up the lines of communication so the impact of the casino on adjacent communities could be brought out in the open and discussed.

When we "went public" with our intent to open a casino, all hell broke loose. The telephone at the State Gaming Commission Office in Olympia rang off the hook. Mail arrived by the box load, and the Commission Office fax machine spit out citizen commentary by the ream. The State contacted us. They said that since there was such an unexpected civic outcry that a public hearing might best serve everyone's interests. We were the only tribe in the state required to hold a public hearing. The hearing was not to seek the public's approval to open the casino. The hearing was just meant to alleviate some of the community concerns.

Two hundred and fifty folks packed themselves like sardines into the Poulsbo Fire Hall. The debate was spirited to say the least. The Upland Property Owners of Washington and the wealthy Whites living on leased tribal waterfront property showed up in force. An entourage of county officials accompanied them. Community concerns ran the gamut from fear of drugs and prostitution to complaints that the tribe was exempt from paying federal income tax on their employees.

I recognized a young lady at that gathering. She had graduated from high school a year in front of me. She was very outspoken . . . a cheerleader for the concerns of the community. She was also a cheerleader in high school so, as you can imagine, she knew how to rally support. Her father was also very outspoken about Tribal involvement with the casino. He was one of those folks with a nice waterfront home in front of Agate Pass. He was involved in the lawsuit over shellfish harvesting rights on the eleven miles of tidelands.

I ran into that same gal at the Casino one night after it had opened. I asked her how she felt about the casino and if it was as bad as she had pictured it. She told me that she was surprised by how busy the place was. She also said that we needed to do something about the cigarette smoke but that everything else was good. The Suquamish Tribe is now one of the largest employers in Kitsap County, though our success wasn't a cakewalk. We suffered through a steep learning curve.

I started getting phone calls from folks I knew in the community, folks who knew me personally . . . folks who were distributors and wholesalers to the casino. They were calling me up to complain, "You know your guys haven't paid us yet." I felt obligated to call up the casino manager and yell at him to "Pay the goddamn bill!" I had to do that on several occasions. My reputation was hanging out there.

The casino manager at the time was also overseeing bingo. I asked him how many seats he had to fill at a bingo session to break even. I knew that the number was sixty-three. He said he didn't know. I asked him how many slices of tomato he got out of one tomato when he was making sandwiches for lunch; how many drinks he got out of a fifth of whiskey; how many people had been showing up for bingo? He said he didn't know . . . didn't have a clue. I told him that it was his job to know that sixty-three seats must be filled to break even. I told him to go look it up and give me a call when he had it figured out. I gave him my unlisted home phone number. I asked him not to share it with anyone because I was still getting hate calls at home. I never got that phone call from him.

I looked at the structure of the casino . . . when we opened and when we closed. They were running two shifts, days and swing. I asked the casino manager what the drop was on dayshift, the drop being when you pull in all of the money and count it. He couldn't tell me . . . just gave me a blank look. He told me that he was just doing one drop each day at the end of the night. I asked him how he could possibly know if there was any value associated with the hours we were working if he didn't do a drop at the end of each shift.

I went to security and I got the attendance numbers. The security folks have little clickers. They walk around and just count heads. I wanted to see when the people were in the casino. I had them do a count every hour. They started counting the minute we opened. I had them drop at the end of day shift and drop at the end of swing shift. When I got the drop figures and the count, I could see the bell curve. I told the casino manager that, based on my calculations, we should open up three hours later. We could stagger employee working hours, and nobody would lose an hour of pay. That simple change would save around $300,000 annually. The guy ignored me. I finally got him relieved, but it was over a whole other issue.

The casino had a three-year contract on the loan for start-up fees. We were holding our own and were only nine months away from paying that loan off and being debt free—only nine more months of carrying a debt load of $800,000 a month. By the interest rates of the 1997–1998 timeframe, we could have supported an eight-million-dollar loan based on our payouts. We had also accumulated $475,000 in unpaid debt from our vendors—the folks who provided the casino with food, alcohol, signs, printing, you name it.

The tribe was looking at restructuring our loan package so we could see more revenue up front. I was really torn. I wanted someone to explain to me why we shouldn't just carry that debt load for nine months and be completely out from under it. I wanted to know why we should refinance. We ended up refinancing. We got sold a bill of goods by a fast-talking refinancier. We should have gone with the nine more months. That was another bad decision made by our Board. They restructured and consolidated debt, and now I have no idea how far they are from paying it off.

The casino is a profitable enterprise. People come to the casino to gamble, have fun, and be entertained. It's no secret that the odds favor the house. Many people walk away with extra money in their pocket, but over a period of time, the house will always come out on top. The profit covers a healthy payroll. There is enough money to hire quality entertainment and furnish clientele with good food and liquor. There is enough money to fund the needs of the tribal community. There is also enough money to test the resolve of those who are entrusted with the responsibility to determine how that money should be spent.

29 | The Vision

AS TRIBAL CHAIRMAN, I KNEW THAT THERE WERE MANY TRIBAL members who didn't own property on the reservation. I felt that we should give them a place to call home. I proposed that we buy property for tribal housing. I knew that with the casino up and running that we could offer those folks employment and upward mobility. The Tribal Council saw the vision but they lacked the courage to follow through.

I envisioned a college campus on the reservation. Education was one of our highest priorities. I went to Olympic Community College and offered up twenty-five acres on the reservation where they could build an extension campus. The curriculum could focus on hotel management, fisheries biology, tourism, the culinary arts, the fine arts, and traditional Northwest art.

I met with the Board of Regents at Olympic College. We discussed differences and issues we had with their plan to put an Olympic College campus on twenty-five acres in Poulsbo at the site of the Olhava Development. Olhava is a 250 to 300-acre tract just north of town where the developers plan to put in a mall complex. The tribe came out against Olhava. The project will have a direct impact on Dogfish Creek, which flows into Liberty Bay. Dogfish Creek is a Chinook salmon stream. I felt that the folks at the Olhava Development offered to donate twenty-five acres to Olympic College to make the development project more palatable to the general public. The development itself would be like a rider on a bill promising a community a college extension campus. I feel it's a ruse, a smoke screen. The developers aren't interested in providing educational benefits to the community. They offered development land for an extension campus as a way to grease the skids during the permit process. Those folks are going to clear-cut and build a huge mall complex that will impact everything from traffic to utilities to salmon survival, but hell, they did promise us a college extension campus!

I thought that if the tribe could snatch away the college campus, Olhava's crown jewel, we could get the development shut off. There is no question in my mind that the Olhava Development will have an adverse impact on the Chinook salmon run in Dogfish Creek. Those salmon are endangered. Where and when do we draw the line? I'm afraid that Mother Nature will eventually draw the line for us.

I went to see the Board of Trustees at Olympic College. I offered them a way for us to settle our differences. We could be the first tribe in the state, if not the nation, with a Community College Extension Campus. I offered up twenty-five acres of reservation land for one dollar a year. I told them that we probably would want twenty-five books and tuitions paid for and some input as to how the courses were structured. We knew the lay of the land. We knew where the campus could be built. The state would assist us in providing the infrastructure to complete the work because it would be a state-funded community college.

While reviewing transportation issues, we discovered an old statute that talked about the railroad. One of our legal minds suggested that we strike it. I protested. I told the Council that with that statute in place, we could get right of ways for our railroad. With a functional railroad we could create a port that would provide the tribe with revenue. Again, the thinking of the Council was very closed minded.

I looked into building a Federal Firefighter Training Center on the reservation where we could train cadets for our own Fire Department. I contracted some Fire folks from Puget Sound Naval Shipyard to come by and inspect our buildings. The inspectors reported that the seat of our tribal government was on its ass . . . a public building with out-of-date fire extinguishers, piggy-backed electrical cords, you name it. We were in bad shape . . . couldn't even maintain a national fire standard in our own building. I insisted that we clean up our act and then use the tax base that the county was receiving from each of those twenty-five-foot lots within the bounds of the Port Madison Indian Reservation to provide local fire service just like any other legitimate municipality. As it is now, there is a two-to six-month waiting period for cadets just to get into firefighter training. That was another one of my visions that went away when I resigned as chairman.

I also proposed that our tribal fishermen remove the net drums from their boats and replace them with ten-pole holders. Get the nets off the water. Net fishing destroys the habitat. The average tribal fisherman today makes, rough guess, around $20,000 a year. The tribe takes five percent of that, or $1000. I proposed that the tribe issue tribal fishing licenses to non-Indians at $3.00 per person for a 72-hour period. The folks buying the licenses would be required to go out fishing on one of our tribal-member-owned chartered fishing boats. We could charge $50.00 per person for a day of fishing, and the fish that were caught would count against the tribal fifty percent.

The tribe would get the revenue from each $3 license plus five percent of each tribal fisherman's gross income. I went to the casino when it first opened up. I asked them if they thought their hotel guests would enjoy charter-boat fishing for salmon. The folks at the casino thought that was a great idea. They figured they could bring in high rollers from the Midwest and treat them to a day of salmon fishing and a night of shooting craps and playing cards. The casino thought they could keep five boats full at all times. That adds up to around fifty people each day that we could take fishing.

I presented the idea to the Tribal Council. "This is simple math," I explained. "I'll talk real slow so you can keep up. At $3 for a license, the tribe would make $30 with every boatload." I looked around to make sure I saw heads nodding up and down. "The charter-boat captain would make $50 a head, or around $500 a day. You could go out twice a day, morning bite and the evening bite. Twenty people times $50 is $1,000 a day, right?" Heads nodded up and down. "Can we do it a hundred days a year? You bet. That's $100,000 a year for each tribal fisherman . . . and oh, by the way, the casino will fill the boats up for you . . . guaranteed. Is there anything wrong with that?"

Their response, "It's not our traditional way of fishing."

"Well," I said, "you each made $20,000 last year, and it cost you $17,000 to run your boat! You're netting $3,000. How smart is that? You can make that much money in only three days of fishing my way and we could get the nets off the water. It doesn't stop there," I explained. "We go down to the Reservation Hatchery where we have chum carcasses that we can't give away, and we build a commercial smokehouse. Every chum or King that comes up that creek, we snag it, milk it or get the eggs, and we smoke it. Good tasting stuff. We get this high roller from the Midwest. The casino pays us $50 to take him fishing, and if he doesn't catch any fish, we hand him a commercially smoked, vacuum-sealed chum or Chinook carcass. We tell him, 'We're sorry the fishing was poor. We know you didn't catch anything, but here's a $40 piece of smoked salmon just for participating in this fishery with us.' Are those folks going to come back? You bet. Are they going to tell their friends? What do you think? What have we lost and what have we gained?"

The Tribal Council's response, "It's not our traditional way of fishing."

I've already found a ten-pole charter boat that I plan on buying. I'm going to go jump up and down on Tribal Council's desk and tell them I want a tribal permit to take these folks fishing. I'm going to do it myself. I'll cut a deal with the casino and put in a commercial smoker behind the lodge at Eagle Tree RV. I'll do it myself and they can all kiss my ass.

30 | Self-Governance

CONGRESS FUNDS INDIAN RESERVATIONS ACROSS THE COUNTRY. They allocate a chunk of money, which trickles down to the individual Indian tribes through the Department of the Interior's Bureau of Indian Affairs. Headquarters for the Bureau of Indian Affairs is in Washington, D.C., and there are regional and area offices of the Bureau across the country. The regional office for the Suquamish, as well as thirty-six other recognized tribes in the northwest portion of the United States, is located in the town of Everett in Washington state. There are twelve area offices of the Bureau. The Indian tribes in Washington state, parts of Idaho, Oregon, and Northern California are affiliated with the area office in Portland, Oregon.

There are well over ten thousand civil servants working for the Bureau, and it's no secret to the Indians that the entire organization is brimming with corruption, fraud and incompetence. Only a small fraction of the money filtered through the Bureau of Indian Affairs to each Indian tribe actually makes it to its intended destination.

Secretary Bruce Babbitt, the Department of the Interior's cabinet member under Clinton, selected an Indian woman, Ada Deer, to be the Director of Indian Affairs. I attended a reception for Ada in the Senate Building when she was confirmed. Washington, D.C., throws receptions like you wouldn't believe. You could go back there and eat free for weeks just by showing up at the receptions. Ada handed me her commemorative coin at that reception. If I were a better shot, I'd blow a hole in that coin. Political appointments are made the way chess pieces are moved on a chessboard. The idea is to maintain the checks and balances by countering one viewpoint with another. The truth is often found somewhere in the middle. It was no secret to me, or anyone else for that matter, that Ada Deer was inept at best. Her appointment by Secretary Babbitt as Director of Indian Affairs was meant to tip the political scales. Fortunately, her glaring shortcomings and poor performance resulted in her removal from that position. Unfortunately, Ada did not disappear.

Congress established a National Gaming Commission whose charter it is to monitor Indian Gaming and insure that the games are legitimate and everything is on the up and up. There are three seats on the Commission . . . one seat filled by the Democrats, one seat by the Republicans, and one seat is filled by an appointment from the Secretary of the Interior.

Under Clinton, Richard Hope, Bob Hope's son from California, filled the Republican seat. Martha Brown Feather, a very knowledgeable and well-educated Indian woman filled the Democratic seat. So, what does Secretary of the Interior, Mr. Babbitt do? He picks Ada Deer to occupy the vacant seat on the Gaming Commission. The Commission ends up split on every issue.

The Department of Justice, the Environmental Protection Agency, and Housing and Urban Development also have tribal offices. Terry Williams from the Tulalip Tribe in Everett was selected to head up the Office for Indian Affairs for the EPA. Terry spent two years back in D.C. and eventually resigned. He said he felt overwhelmed by the bureaucracy. Housing and Urban Development doesn't have the controls or the checks and balances they need. A few years back, the General Manager of the Tulalip Reservation Casino completed an application for a HUD low-income house. He also had five members of his family submit separate applications. When the HUD money showed up, they pooled their money and built one hell of a nice big house. They got busted.

Washington State Senator Slade Gorton, to demonstrate how screwed up the Indians were, made sure that the *Seattle Post-Intelligencer* was reprinted the next morning to include that story. Slade arranged for a copy of the paper to be placed on the doorstep of every United States Congressman and Senator. Slade Gorton is no friend to the Indians. Slade was the Washington State Attorney General in 1974 when the state lost the Bolt decision and the tribes were awarded fifty percent of the salmon harvest. The Bolt decision had a rippling effect throughout the United States. The treaty rights of the East Coast Indians also impacted his family's fishing business. Slade's family owns Gorton's Fisherman, the company that makes frozen fishsticks.

When the Democrats controlled the Senate, Senator Daniel Inouye from Hawaii was appointed as the chairman of the Senate Committee for Indian Affairs. In the recent Republican sweep, the Democrats lost the majority in the Senate, so the Republicans decided they would appoint Senator Gorton as the Chairman of the Senate Committee for Indian Affairs. There was a great uprising. Many felt putting Slade Gorton in that position would be like putting David Duke of the Ku Klux Klan in charge of the NAACP and comparisons like that were being used.

The Republicans then took Ben Night Horse Campbell, who was a Democrat-turned-Republican from Colorado, and moved him into the Senate Committee for Indian Affairs. We're thinking that was a good thing. On one side of the spectrum you have Slade Gorton, and on the other side you have Ben Night Horse Campbell with a cadre of individuals in between. Ben Night Horse is the answer to Slade Gorton. He represents the Indian viewpoint. The political checks and balances appeared to be in place. Appearances are sometimes deceiving.

The tribes in the Pacific Northwest often take a leadership role on national issues. Several of us decided to go back to D.C. and have an audience with Senator Campbell. I went, as did Billy Frank from the Nisqually, who was the Northwest Indian Fisheries Commission Chairman. Chairman Ron Allen of the Jamestown S'Klallam, who was President of the National Congress of American Indians, was with us. Henry Cagie from the Lummi Nation and Dale Resling, Chairman of the Hoopla Tribe of Northern California, also went along.

The five of us made arrangements to have dinner with Senator Campbell. After dinner, we planned to sequester ourselves in the Senator's office and openly discuss Indian issues. When we got to D.C., we called his office to let him know we were in town and that we would meet him for dinner the next day. His Chief of Staff and some other flunky showed up for dinner ... he sent his boys. We told his Chief of Staff to tell the Senator that we were going to meet with him in his office at 3:00 the next day. The flunky says, "I'm sorry, but the Senator is very busy and you'll need a reservation."

We said, "No, we don't need an appointment, the Senator knew we were coming, and the Senator knows we are here, and we're gonna sit in his office until we can see him."

We all arrived at his office at around three o'clock the next day. We spent probably an hour and a half looking at his beautiful Indian regalia and Indian artwork hanging on the walls. The Senator finally showed up and said, "Gentlemen, I've got five minutes."

Billy Frank has always been a man who speaks his piece. He has addressed the United Nations and the World Trade Council regarding Indian rights. Billy says, "Senator, you represent us, and we'll take as much time as we need." We all went into his office and closed the door.

The first thing that came out of the Senator's mouth was, "You gentlemen don't realize I need to raise $5,000 a day just to get re-elected in two years." We were there to discuss Indian rights, and our representative . . . our vote . . . is telling us how much money he needs to win reelection in two years.

Things deteriorated for me after that statement. "Senator," I said, "you are our voice. You are our answer, our counter to Slade Gorton. People are going to hear Slade's words and expect you to speak to our concerns. That way folks will draw some kind of reasonable conclusion, hopefully in the middle someplace."

The honorable Senator Ben NO Horse Campbell says, "You didn't hear me. I've got to raise $5,000."

This guy's got a beautiful, full-length, war bonnet in his office. He's got Navajo sand paintings under glass . . . beautiful jewelry, tomahawks, awards, a photo of him riding his pinto pony . . . everything is very rustic. "Senator," I said, "you are our voice, and from what I've heard of your voice so far, you don't have the right to have this regalia in your office. You are not who we thought you were. You do not represent the Indian people of this nation!" I was boiling mad at that point. I got up and stormed out of his office, slamming the door behind me.

Billy Frank rushed out after me. "Jesus, Lyle, I've never seen you so pissed. That guy really rubbed you the wrong way."

The Senator didn't care about our concerns. He could care less about what we needed back home. He was only worried about getting re-elected. And so it goes, a complete dereliction of duty.

Senator Ben NO Horse Campbell was re-elected, and Senator Gorton was fortunately removed from the Senate Committee for Indian Affairs. Unfortunately, he was given a more prestigious Senate Committee. They moved him to Appropriations . . . they gave Slade the purse strings.

One of our Suquamish tribal members, who had been living in California, was selected to fill a high level job with the Bureau of Indian Affairs. When we got word of his appointment, we considered it a great stroke of luck. There was a Suquamish tribal member holding a high-ranking, influential position with the Bureau. I called him up.

"This is Emerson George. I'm your Tribal Chairman. I'd like to come out and visit. Where are you located?"

He was very receptive. He said he was glad to hear from me and he invited me back to D.C. He said that he occupied the corner office at the end on the top floor of the Department of Interior Building. The Interior Building covers an entire city block. Our guy was on the top floor, in a corner office! I was very excited about meeting this influential fellow.

I arrived in D.C a day early, checked into my room, picked up a bite to eat, and took a tour of the town. I found I could walk into the Senate Building, the House Building, the Capitol Building, the Capitol Rotunda, and the House and Senate Chambers simply by passing through a metal detector and having my briefcase x-rayed.

The next morning, when I showed up at the Department of the Interior Building and tried to enter, I was stopped at the door. The guard asked me to show two pieces of picture ID. He asked me who I was going to visit, which floor I was going to, and exactly how long I planned to be there. I'm thinking, "Damn, this is really a big wheel!"

The first floor hallway was very busy with people rushing about carrying briefcases and papers. I stepped into the elevator and pressed #3 on the keypad. The elevator stopped, the doors opened, and I walked into an empty hallway . . . dead quiet. It was like a ghost town. His office was supposedly located in the southwest corner so I meandered in that general direction. My footsteps echoed off the walls. I walked through a large door and into a large reception area. There was no one there. The place was completely empty except for a small pile of cardboard boxes pushed up against one wall. In the far corner of the reception area was an office door. This guy's name was on the door, and the lights were on. I walked over, knocked, and heard someone stirring inside. The door opened so fast it startled me. He grabbed my hand and shook it so hard my fingers went numb.

"Mr. George, Mr. George," he gushed, "come in, come in, please, come in." The guy was so excited I thought he was gonna pee on me. "You're the first visitor I've had in the last three months," he said. "Come on in and have a seat. Here let me bring you a chair. How is everything back home? Can I get you something—coffee, soda?"

"Nice office," I said, still somewhat stunned. "Everything back home is as good as can be expected."

I looked around the room. Nothing was the way I had envisioned. The place was small and there were piles of paper in every corner. The guy had a desk by the window and even that was buried in paper. I'm not sure he ever threw anything away.

"Tell me," I said. "What exactly do you do for the Bureau?"

"I'm one of their auditors," he said.

"No kidding," I replied. "So, how's the auditing business?"

"Oh," he said, "the auditing business is not too good right now. We get scrutinized pretty hard. We can't find three of the four dollars that Congress gives us to distribute to the tribes."

I wasn't sure I heard him right. "Excuse me, what was that again?"

"The money," he said. "We can't find seventy-five percent of the funding allocated by Congress to the Bureau for distribution to the tribes."

I couldn't believe what I had just heard.

"What do you mean you can't find it?" I said.

"Can't find it," he continued, kind of matter-of-factly. "Can't substantiate where that money has gone. Nobody can account for it."

What I was hearing is that seventy-five percent of the tribe's funding disappears into the black hole of the Bureau. We never see it.

Indian tribes submit their wish-lists to the Bureau of Indian Affairs prior to the start of each fiscal year. Until recently, money was allocated to each Indian tribe via the Bureau, and expenditures were controlled and tracked via line-item budget. The line-item budget was pretty straightforward. Each item on the tribe's wish-list was funded individually. For example, if the tribe identified a need for two new computers and a new fisheries truck on their wish-list, then money would be earmarked in the tribe's annual budget specifically for the purchase of those items. By law, the tribe was not allowed to spend that money in any other way. So, under the constraints of a line-item budget, should some emergent need arise, we did not have the leeway, or even the option, to redirect that funding.

Suquamish community members were suffering for the want of basic services. There were pregnant tribal women who couldn't afford maternity care. There were children in need of dental work. There were elders who couldn't pay their power bills. My telephone would ring off the hook with angry folks demanding to know why we had purchased two new computers and why the Chief of the Tribal Fisheries Department was driving around town in a shiny new truck. As Tribal Chairman, I was the one they called. I was the man. The buck stopped with me. I didn't blame them for being upset. Not only were we being shorted seventy-five percent of our funding, the line-items that were approved for funding did not address many of our critical needs, and by law, our hands were tied. I can't count how many hours I spent trying to explain that issue to angry and frustrated community members.

At the time, I was a member of the National Congress of American Indians ... a Congressman for lack of a better word. The National Congress appointed an Executive Body. Their charter was to serve as a clearinghouse for proposed legislation that could impact Indian tribes across the country. The Executive Body convened twice a year for ten-day sessions.

Northwest tribal leaders, myself included, knew that we needed to take things into our own hands. We took the lead in the fight for self-governance. We knew it was time to convince congressional lawmakers that Indian tribes were smart enough to run their own business, free from the suffocating bureaucracy of the Bureau of Indian Affairs, free from line-item restrictions, and free from the regulatory controls of the Government Man.

We brought our self-governance proposal to the Executive Body of National Congress, and they ushered the self-governance legislation into Congress. Our plan was relatively simple. Under self-governance, we would go out into our communities and ask our people to identify their issues and concerns ... education, housing, welfare, community health, buying back reservation land, you name it. Armed with community input, we would prioritize our needs and put together blocks, grants and contracts for presentation to Congress. Congress would then allocate funding to our tribal governments via the newly established Self-Governance Office in Washington, D.C., bypassing the money-sucking bureaucracy of the Bureau of Indian Affairs.

The self-governance legislation met with a great deal of opposition. There were those in the Bureau of Indian Affairs who were quite anxious about the prospect of losing such a large cash cow. Under self-governance, the tribes would handle their own education, housing, forestry, fisheries, and health-care needs. There would no longer be a need for most, if not all, of the bureaucrats working for the Bureau of Indian Affairs. Many politicians considered it unwise to support legislation that could eliminate thousands of civil service jobs, especially if the direct impact on their constituency would threaten their plans for re-election.

The self-governance proposal also had strong support. The reduction of big government was in favor at the time. There was a concerted lobbying effort put forth toward passage. Many saw self-governance as a way to eliminate unnecessary civil service jobs while actually improving the cost and quality of services provided to the tribes. Senator John McCain from Arizona, well known amongst the tribes as a friend of the Indians, and Senator Daniel Inouye from Hawaii were instrumental in shepherding the legislation through the Senate. I was personally afforded the opportunity of visiting the office of Senator Inouye. Chief Sealth's speech is hanging on the wall behind his desk. The Senator recognized me as a descendant of Chief Sealth, which I considered a great honor.

The Self-Governance Legislation was passed in 1989. Ten tribes were selected to participate in the pilot program. The Suquamish Tribe was among those selected. Each tribe received a $150,000 planning grant to help move them into a self-governance mode. The tribes were given a timeline to accomplish certain tasks. That was the non-Indian side . . . task oriented . . . making sure that the foundation was in place and that each department had its budget. We hired a person to act as our Self-governance Coordinator, someone to help set up our budgeting process. We sent that person to training with some of the money from the planning grant.

The dynamics of self-governance are pretty straight forward. The tribe identifies its needs. Congress allocates sufficient funding to satisfy those needs, and the tribe decides where and how to spend that money. Our Community Development folks went out into the community with a questionnaire. We held public hearings to identify our primary issues. The needs of our people would no longer be identified in Portland or Everett or 3000 miles away in Washington, D.C. We would no longer have to depend on the Great White Father in Washington telling us how and where we must spend our money.

We completely restructured how we did business. The first year of self-governance we rolled over our previous year's grants and contracts to the individual departments: legal, housing, health care, mental health care, physical health care, fisheries, law enforcement, administrative, accounting, community development, and natural resources. We funded each department at the same level as the previous year when we had operated under the line-item budget. The department heads were told that if they desired any changes to their budget, they must bring their issues forward. The Tribal Council, the elected governing body of the Suquamish Nation, would make those budget decisions.

The money to pay for self-governance came from the Bureau of Indian Affairs. The regional and area offices of the Bureau had provided a service to the Indians for x-number of dollars. Bureau headquarters in Washington, D.C., had provided oversight for "x" number of dollars. If the tribes selected for self-governance were now providing those services for themselves, then the various Bureau offices no longer needed that money. The money was redirected from the Bureau to the tribes.

The self-governance pilot program was relatively successful. There are now fifty tribes, representing about ten percent of the federally recognized tribes across the United States and Alaska, participating in the self-governing compact. Some tribes have been very successful with self-government. Locally, the Jamestown S'Klallam Tribe has done quite well. Ron Allen, of the Jamestown S'Klallam served two years as Chairman of the National Council. He was also Chairman of the Seven Cedars Casino. Had Senator John McCain won the Republican nomination for president in the year 2000, and then carried the November election, I feel that Ron Allen was in an excellent position to have been selected for the position of Undersecretary of the Interior for the Bureau of Indian Affairs.

Today, the Bureau of Indian Affairs is still layered in bureaucracy. They handle the financial affairs of the large majority of Indian tribes not yet chosen for self-governance. Politicians looking for a way to cut out the fat are starting to do the math. Ten percent of the tribes are in the self-governance pilot program and only eight bureaucrats are watching the store. Simple math would suggest that if all of the recognized tribes in the country were in the self-governance compact, then only eighty civil servants could run the show.

Self-governance is the essence of our people. Self-governance ensures our sovereignty. Self-governance gives us the ability to determine and fulfill tribal needs, the power to plan for our future, the tools to rise above poverty and addiction, and the opportunity to realize our visions. I was ready and willing to lead that quest, but it was not to be.

31 | The Turning of the Tide

I FIRST NOTICED THE WHEELS COMING OFF THE CART IN THE summer of 1997. Our department heads were told that their funding would be based solely on the priorities established by the tribal community, even if that meant moving $300,000 from the fisheries budget into housing. We followed that plan to the letter for the first half of the year.

During our review of the next year's budget, we knew that we faced some hard decisions. We would need to make cuts in some of our programs. We planned to offset part of the 1997 budget with tribal hard dollars. Hard dollars are a separate bucket of money from our own enterprises. Hard dollars are not renewable; once you spend them, they're gone. The revenue we received from the property that Mr. Jones leased from the tribe went into that bucket. The revenue from fireworks' licensing also went into the bucket.

I know there are many folks who believe that Indians sell illegal fireworks on the reservation, but that is simply not true. Fireworks distributors on the reservation pay the tribe a fee to sell their fireworks. The fireworks are Legal Class 3 fireworks and remain legal as long as they stay on the reservation. If you purchase fireworks from us and set them off while you're still on the reservation, you have not broken any laws.

The wholesalers who provide our fireworks are all licensed through the state. You can bet they pay state taxes on the revenue that they generate. The fireworks that are available off of the reservation are distributed by an outfit out of Tacoma.

It has a large warehouse, about twelve acres, and it sells the "safe and sane" fireworks.

I will say that there are individuals who use the Indians to peddle illegal fireworks . . . some guy in his garage making M-80s, M-100s and M-1000s. That is individual proprietorship, and I know for a fact that it does exist. My stance on those fireworks is that they are a violation of tribal law and should not be allowed on our reservation. It concerns me that neither our Police Department nor our Tribal Court system has the balls to actively pursue that issue.

Tribal hard dollars also come from the tribe's commercial harvesting of shellfish. In 1997, our tribal biologist projected that we would take in around a million dollars in revenue from our geoduck harvest during fiscal year 1998. That is where the trouble began. The Tribal Council voted to commit two-thirds of that projected revenue for fisheries enhancement and enforcement. They voted to spend money we didn't have yet, on a departmental budget that had not been identified as a tribal priority by the community. They were robbing Peter, who didn't have a dime in his pocket, to pay Paul, who was planning to spend $600,000 of imaginary money so a few fishermen could improve their lot in life.

When I first got on the Tribal Council, I was my own mind. I spoke my own piece. I wasn't afraid to tell anybody and everybody what I thought of any issue. I felt my role was different as Tribal Council Chairman. I chaired the meetings and set the agenda. I had a voice, but I only voted when there was a tie. I felt it was my responsibility to share my visions with the six voting Council members. I felt that I could influence their thinking on key issues.

I strongly protested when the Council voted to commit that projected income. I proposed that it was time to move forward under self-governance. It was time to build some order and continuity into our infrastructure. I explained to the Council members that they could still fish, that they still had that right, but under no circumstances should we spend $600,000 on a fisheries enhancement and enforcement program that at best would only return around five cents for ever dollar we spent. They wanted to spend $600,000 dollars so twelve fishermen could catch $30,000 worth of salmon. That made absolutely no sense and was in direct violation of the basic principles of self-governance.

As a result of productive salmon runs and a fair price at the market, each of our commercial fishermen averaged $80,000 dollars in 1988. Those same fishermen averaged only $20,000 from 1995 through 1997. As a compromise, I suggested that we use $240,000 of that projected revenue to pay our twelve fishermen not to fish. We could pay them to not fish just like the government pays farmers to not grow tobacco. That would still leave about $360,000 that we could use to re-educate those fishermen, to teach them a new skill. Some of the fishermen are elders. The geoduck money would go a long way towards helping them take better care of themselves. With that kind of money we could provide health care for our people, including our fishermen, who couldn't seem to manage their money well enough to afford insurance. Health care was one of our identified tribal priorities.

I lobbied Council members. I called up our vice-chairman and explained to him that I needed his support on the issue of deficit spending and misappropriation of funds. I discussed these issues with the treasurer, vice-chairman, and the secretary. I got their word that I had their support. I talked to one of the General Council members and he said he was with me. He promised his support. I remember looking directly at him at our next meeting. He was sitting at the end of the table. A motion was made to direct any revenue from the harvest of geoduck to fill tribal needs. I asked for a yea or nay vote. I looked directly at him and I saw the change . . . this guy who had given me his commitment . . . this guy who had said he was behind me one-hundred percent . . . this guy who told me he could see where I was headed and he thought I had the right idea. He voted no. He went against his word. I was dumbfounded. I looked him in the eye and he turned away, not because of his culture, but because of his shame. His word means nothing to me now . . . doesn't mean two cents when it comes down to making the right decision.

The fishermen were adamant about their fishing rights. They refused to stay off the water. They insisted that fishing was their heritage and their cultural right. They could not hear my words. I never suggested that they couldn't fish. I had a very ill feeling. The fishermen were mad as hell at me for my stand against spending projected revenue on fisheries and enhancement. I had over 800 people to worry about. My concerns were for the folks in the community, not with twelve fishermen.

I told the Council that if they stood by their decision to commit projected geoduck revenue to the Fisheries Department, then I would resign my position as chairman. I told them that I wanted nothing to do with the path they were taking.

I wanted the community to see that their Tribal Council was leading them down a death spiral path. I wanted the community to understand that those were tribal geoducks . . . that the revenue from that resource should be used to support community-driven needs, based on the needs assessment, based on the priorities that the community had laid out for us. Those were the issues that we were obligated to fund, and in that order.

As it ended up, the tribe realized a little over a million dollars in revenue from the geoduck harvest. The Tribal Council was gracious enough to put forty percent of that money into tribal programs . . . after I resigned. A Tribal Council member called me at home to point out the success of the geoduck harvest. He attempted to convince me that everything had worked out, that it was okay that they had spent that money up front. "No harm, no foul," he said. I told him that if a man runs a stop sign and doesn't hit anyone that it doesn't mean he did the right thing. The bottom line did not change. Two-thirds of the geoduck revenue was improperly allocated to the fisheries program in direct contradiction of the principles of self-governance.

Overall, I figure we pissed away just shy of a million dollars in 1998, based on the $600,000 of geoduck revenue that was misappropriated plus the $300,000 we wasted on mismanagment of our Class 3 gaming operation. All of that money could have, and should have, been applied to the identified tribal needs. In my opinion, self-governance on the Suquamish Reservation is not working. Someone is going to say that the Indians are incapable of handling their own affairs, and I'm afraid I have to agree.

My concern and frustration was not limited to the geoduck issue. After hours of deliberation, the Tribal Council would make a solid decision. We would all agree that "by God this is it," and we're gonna live with it. Community members would show up in arms at the very next Tribal Council meeting. They would scream, holler, yell, jump up and down, threaten us within an inch of our lives, and tell us that we'll never get reelected again. The Council members would buckle under and reverse themselves. I tried to explain to them that important decisions must not be made based on political pressure. I told them we needed to make decisions that were right for the tribe and then stand behind them. That didn't happen . . . still isn't happening. Our credibility is nonexistent.

Years ago, the Suquamish Tribal Government established the Port Madison

Enterprise Board. The Board served to advise the tribe on important issues. Four Tribal Council members were on the Board. We also had participation by many influential community leaders. Realtor Reid Scott was on the Board. Ron Ross of Ross Development, who owns Ross Plaza, was on the Board. We had the senior vice-president of North Sound Bank on our Board for a number of years. His office is decorated with traditional Northwest art that he purchased from our artisans . . . paid good money for it. Those non-Indian, business-oriented folks helped steer our Enterprise Board. There recently was a lot of turmoil on the Board. I stepped in as Council Chairman to help weather the storm.

What did I hear? "Get them damn White guys off that Board! What are they doing on our Enterprise Board?"

I told the Indian Board members that I felt we already had too many Indians running the show. I told them that many of those non-Indian Board members were more Indian than they were! They brought to the table more business sense learned in their lifetime than half of us in the group will probably ever get! They wanted them off the Board because they were non-Indian? That made absolutely no sense to me at all. I fought a constant battle with those types of dynamics.

I challenged one of our elders at the Council meeting the night of the insurrection of our Police Department. I asked him to explain to me why he was there. I asked him if he had heard anything that I had said. I asked him if he listened to my point of view; did he understand that I was trying to bring some center to the discussion.

He told me that he didn't hear all of what I had said, but he had heard Pete say this, and Pete say that, and he knew that Pete was right because Pete got up and screamed and hollered and cussed.

I could have had many of those folks that night arrested for threatening us with anarchy and violence. Billy Walks Backwards was there, of course, as was a fellow I referred to as "The Trickster". I'm not sure if he was an enrolled member of any tribe, though he professed to be an Indian wiseman, some kind of spiritual leader. I know he used peyote in his ceremonies, which is not a traditional Northwest Indian custom, and causes me to question the wiseman moniker. The Suquamish Indian Church also uses peyote, which is against everything that I stand for . . . everything that our culture stands for.

The insurrections of the Police Department and our Enterprise Board, deficit spending, misappropriation of tribal hard dollars, threats to my family, were all contributing factors to my resignation. Drug-testing for staff and Tribal Council members was another hard spot with me. We had a policy in place that required us to operate in an alcohol and drug-free work environment. Every grant and contract that I signed, including my endorsement of the 2.5 million dollar self-governance check, was based on that premise. It was simply not true. We were not clean. As far as I was concerned, we were accepting Federal money on an annual basis under false pretenses.

I was swimming upstream against a powerful current, and I was alone. I could no longer fight the flow. While I was on the Tribal Council, I was only able to enjoy a week of leave with my family on an annual basis. I was constantly on the move trying to drum up money, or I was interviewing somebody, or I was dealing with creditors, or I was off trying to arrange financing for the casino. I traveled back to D.C. several times a year. As a represntative on the National Congress, I attended the weeklong National Congress of Indians Convention, whenever and wherever it was being held. Tribal business took up every minute of my time outside of my regular job. I was seldom home, and when I was, I was on the phone. My family suffered dearly.

I know there are many folks in the community who want me back on the Enterprise Board and the Tribal Council. I'm not interested. I'm not going to put myself, or my family, through that again. There would have to be a complete reseating of the Tribal Council, and even then I'm not sure it's something I would consider. The tribe is in dire need of forward-thinking folks . . . people with the resolve to stand firm by their convictions . . . people who aren't afraid to kick some ass . . . some political ass . . . people who won't worry about pissing off a few fishermen.

The Federal Government, in my opinion, has created nations within nations, full of anarchy and a lack of leadership. There is a lot of money to be had here . . . big money. Enlightened folks with the courage to follow their visions apparently pose a threat to someone's fat pocketbook. Mrs. Donner may not have been too far off. Maybe I didn't give her enough credit for her wisdom. Either way, it's just one more weave in the basket that helps to create holes in the system.

The corruptions of the world have found their way onto our reservation. Cocaine and methamphetamines have been brought in to promote community dysfunction. Rabble rousers have been sent in to foster mistrust, fear and racism. The Osterman case might be a classic example of why that exists. Who has jurisdiction?

Indian tribes are scrutinized to the nth degree. Our credibility is always in jeopardy. Something like this will show just how inept the tribe is at managing our own affairs. For me, addressing these issues on the tribal government side, and then having to go home and deal with those issues in my personal life, has created a lot of internal struggle.

I believed that my concerns and actions as Suquamish Tribal Chairman were rooted in preserving our sovereignty. I know that our tribal elders have a deep understanding of our cultural identity. I listened to their counsel and I tried to learn from their wisdom. I listened to our youth. I tried to identify with their needs. I couldn't speak for our elders. I couldn't speak for our youth. I could speak for our traditional side. All of these things are a part of the same circle. Our youth are our future and our elders are our link to the past. Our traditional ways tie these factions together to make this web of life. If one fragment of that web is disrupted, then the whole web is affected. If the web is not anchored solidly, it will blow with the whisper of the wind.

32 | Eagle Tree RV

I AM DEEPLY TROUBLED BY THE DIRECTION THAT TRIBAL LEADERSHIP has taken our people. I feel that there is nothing more that I can do. I have retired from tribal politics. I feel as though the weight of the world has been lifted from my shoulders. I have found a new focus for my effort and my energy. It feels good to once again be excited and enthusiastic.

Sue and I decided about seven years ago to put all of our efforts into the realization of my father's dream. When Grandmother Martha died, she gifted six-and-one-half acres of land down to my dad. He always wanted to put a mobile home park on that land. Unfortunately, Shady Rest robbed him of his spirit and most of his money. When my dad passed over, he gifted that land to my brother and me. I was gifted 3.3 acres. I purchased an additional 3.3 acres from my paternal aunt.

Sue and I selected an architect in 1995. The architect completed some preliminary drawings, and we opened bids on June 23, 1996, for what would become Eagle Tree RV Park. The park is located just off of highway 305 between Poulsbo and Bainbridge Island. The contractor we selected had bad news. He told us that the existing onsite drain field would not provide adequate drainage. That drain field was supposedly designed for a ten-unit apartment house, a hotel, an eighty-eight-unit RV park, a commercial kitchen, a restaurant, and laundry facilities. Instead of awarding the contract, we decided that it would be smart to obtain an engineering review. The engineer determined that the drain field would probably last Eagle Tree RV six weeks at best. I looked at all of the greenbelts on the property, thinking that something might perk. Nothing worked. We had to redesign and relocate the entire drain field. It is currently located seven-tenths of a mile south of the park, off of George Lane, on a piece of property that my grandma was gifted just to the left of the line between the stump and the tree.

We went to bid a second time in February of 1997. We contacted the bank and informed them that the developers were planning to start the project in three or four days. We told them that we were ready to award the contract. The banker said, "Mr. George, don't sign the contract. I need a couple of days to arrange the financing."

We waited two days and called the bank. The banker told us that they would be unable to give us a loan because the property we were borrowing against was Trust Status property. I couldn't believe what I was hearing. These people knew from day one that we were planning to build on Trust property. They had apparently made no effort to resolve the problem. The banker told us to come back and see him when we had permission to mortgage the property.

Sue and I spent the next three years, from February of 1997 until June of 2000, wading through the bureaucracy of the Bureau of Indian Affairs, trying to get permission to mortgage the property. I initially took our development package to the District Office of the Bureau in Everett. "We don't have the authority to process this, Mr. George," they said. "You're going to have to take it back to the tribe." I told the folks at district that under self-governance the tribe had assumed many responsibilities but that Trust responsibility wasn't on the list.

I called the District Office more times over the next few months than I care to remember. They finally agreed to review our business plan. They said that when they were done with their review the paperwork would have to go to the Regional Office in Portland and then back to Washington, D.C., for final review and approval. Once it was reviewed and approved by Headquarters, it would need to go back to Regional, back to District, and only then could the bank mortgage the property.

We assembled a comprehensive package that included our business plan and a checklist of twelve items. Everything was neatly organized in a three-ring binder, complete with tabs. We even inserted a color title page under the plastic front cover. We spent four thousand dollars on an appraisal. We included a cash flow analysis to show that the park would have a positive cash flow. Everything was there: An anthropological report from the tribe establishing that no bones were found on the property. A section containing a wildlife survey. A report by the Tribal Fisheries

Department indicating there were no year-around streams. A paper stating there would be no adverse impact to wetlands and no eagle roosts or nests would be disturbed. A section showing we had complied with the Endangered Species Act. A page of figures regarding storm water retention as well as an entire segment stating that Sue and I were in good health. Where else, other than through the bureaucracy of the Bureau of Indian Affairs, does a lending institution require an affidavit concerning your health?

I took a Monday off from work and drove to the District Office in Everett. I picked up the business plan and drove down to Portland. I went to lunch with this woman from the Regional Office. The two of us went over the package one line-item at a time. I showed her the three or four sheets that applied to line-item one. I showed her the six sheets that addressed line-item two. We reviewed the entire package page by page.

"Mr. George," she says, "everything looks in order. I will meet with our group on Thursday and we will discuss your business plan. I expect the entire issue to be wrapped up and ready for you to pick up by Friday."

"Okay," I said, "as soon as the package is approved, give me a call. I will fly down and pick it up, personally fly it back to D.C., and get Hilda Manuel at Bureau Headquarters to sign on the dotted line." Hilda and I worked together. We had a good working relationship. "After Hilda signs," I said, "I'll fly the package back to Portland. From there I'll hop a plane back to Seattle and drop it off at the District Office in Everett."

The committee in Portland had their meeting that Thursday. Sue waited until the following Monday to give them a call. The woman wasn't there. Sue left a message but never received a call. Sue called again on Tuesday and left another message. There was still no response. The Portland Office finally called on Wednesday. They told us that our proposal was only the third one that this woman had ever done. Her first was $17,000 on a mobile home. Her second was $39,000 for the purchase of a new home. They apologized. She had never touched anything close to a million dollars. She was in way over her head. Rather than press on and ask for help, she just pushed it aside.

I called the tribe's lobbyist back in D.C. and asked him if there was anyone I could talk to back there who could influence somebody to make a decision. The Chairman of the Lummi Tribe, Henry Cagie, was in the office. I recognized his voice in the background. He was using quite a few expletives with whatever bureaucrat he was yelling at, "There is a Tribal Chairman on the West Coast," he scolded, "who knows what he is doing and what he is talking about. This guy can't get through to you people and he's getting the runaround."

Two days later I got a call from a man in the Everett Office. He said that he now had the authority to make things happen. He told me to bring the paperwork over. I was starting to think that maybe the phone call to Headquarters was actually worth the effort. I took the package to Everett and spent the entire day kissing this guy's ass. He even took me to look at a mobile home park. Apparently, he had seen one once, so he figured he knew what they were all about. He reviewed the package and proudly noted that I had forgotten to include a $400 per month line-item on my spreadsheet for garbage disposal. He told me that I'd have to go home and fix the paperwork error before he could proceed. When I left his office, the guy was grinning from ear to ear.

I corrected the spreadsheet and took him the revised package on February 9, 1999. My job required that I leave the following week for a three-month temporary duty assignment in Pearl Harbor. He said that everything appeared to be in order and that we would have approval to mortgage the property within thirty days. I started calling him from Hawaii on day thirty-one. I burned up a 200-minute phone card trying to get ahold of this guy. I finally got through to him at his Everett office and I was told that he no longer had the authority to get the deal done. He said that the tribe now had the authority, which of course the tribe denied. Sue and I were back to square one.

Sue, who had joined me in Hawaii, flew back home several weeks early to pick up our packet from Everett. Our professional looking business plan, the one with the cover sheet, and the itemized pages complete with tabs, was a mess. There was no three-ring binder, no tabs, and nothing was collated. The papers were all mixed up, crumpled, stained, and stuffed into a manila envelope.

I was telling this nightmare of a story to an acquaintance at work. He told me that his mother-in-law had a White friend who worked in the bureaucracy of Bureau of Indian Affairs. He said that this guy was known to have helped Indians with financial arrangements. I got the guy's phone number and made the call. Sue and I met with him in September of 1999.

This guy said he could guarantee approval from the Bureau for us to secure a loan on our Trust property. His personal services would cost us a small fee of one percent of the entire loan amount. At this point, we were beside ourselves. We gave him our financial package and he read through it. He said that everything seemed to be in order and that he was surprised we had managed to stick with it as long as we had.

Sue and I made a pact with each other that if we didn't have a commitment from the Bureau of Indian affairs by June 1, 2000, we would just sell the property. On the 1st we received written authorization from the Bureau to mortgage the property. Timing is everything, or one percent is. Either way, that's the way it happened, and I never question the way things are.

We toasted our hard-fought victory that night. We had worked so hard for so long. The celebration seemed anti-climactic. We drove downtown to tell the contractor, the guy who had twice started work on the project, that we were finally ready to begin. Construction started on the 2nd of July 2000. Eagle Tree RV opened for business on the 15th of October that same year. I stood alone in the middle of the park on that day and gazed up at the gray sky. I suppose I wanted to give thanks, and in my own way, I wanted to let my dad know that his dream had finally become a reality. An eagle floated over my head. I followed it with my eyes as it effortlessly rode a cushion of air in large graceful circles and then gently landed on the top of a tall cedar tree in the far corner of the park. My father had found a way to tell me that he was pleased.

One piece of the puzzle was all that remained . . . connecting the drainage system at Eagle Tree with the new drain field down on George Drive. We had the permit in hand that would allow us to bore a hole underneath Highway 305. We had been in communication with the Tribal Fisheries Department from the beginning regarding storm-water retention and the type of impermeable surfaces on the property.

I figured that once we put the pipeline under the highway, it would simply be a matter of running a ditch alongside George Lane for the rest of the pipe and hooking the whole business together. I assumed all along, which was almost a fatal mistake on my part, that there was a right-of-way down George Lane. As it turned out there isn't . . . not legally anyway. The first 300 yards is privately owned, and turned out not to be a problem. The next 1,320 feet was an entirely different story. My grandma owned a forty-acre section right in the middle. George Lane has been our driveway since 1956. She buried a well-water transmission line along-side the entire length of that road in 1973, and nobody said a word. In the mid-'80s, the Department of Housing and Urban Development built two low-income houses farther down off of George Lane, and nobody said a word. When we went to dig our little ditch, we were told that we needed to apply for a right-of-way. We were also required to obtain approval signatures from the owners of at least fifty-one percent of the land.

My grandma had gifted that forty-acre parcel to her six children. Subsequently, as each of the six brothers and sisters passed over, their portion of the land was gifted down to their children and grandchildren. Today, sixty-three surviving relatives share ownership of the entire, undivided forty-acre section. The property is very splintered. In fact, to keep track of who owns what, the property has been separated into 9,600 pieces. So, before we made application for a right-of-way, we needed to obtain signatures from the owners of at least fifty-one percent of the pieces.

The landowner with the smallest holdings owned only thirty-five of the 9,600 separate pieces. The biggest single landowner owned five acres, which amounted to over twelve percent of the total pieces or twelve percent of the votes. We got his okay, which was somewhat like carrying California in the presidential election. We eventually managed to get enough signatures to have the fifty-one percent we needed to apply for a right-of-way.

We sent our right-of-way application and the approval signatures to Everett and they said, "We're sorry, you didn't do it right. You didn't get an appraisal. Have an appraisal done. Resubmit your application and then wait for approval from Everett and Portland." We were right back into the perpetual passing of the buck. I really wanted to tell the Bureau that the tribe had jurisdiction over this issue as a part of self-governance. I wanted to tell them that they could kiss my ass. They insisted that I obtain an appraisal of the entire forty-acre parcel as well as a national Environmental Protection Act study to the tune of $3,500. They also insisted that we obtain anthropological and wildlife studies before they would permit us to dig our ditch. They wanted to know the value of the encroachment. They said that my eight-inch line, which would run about 1,520 feet from the highway, represented roughly 1000 square feet of intrusion. The pipe is going to be buried six to twelve feet deep. Where is the intrusion?

The tribe has qualified staff on the Board with the authority and the expertise to determine if there are burial grounds, bones, or any historical gathering sites on that piece of property. He is the same guy that completed the anthropological study for Eagle Tree. All of a sudden, he decides that he doesn't want to get involved. Says he can't do it. Claims it was a conflict of interest because he owns part of the forty acres. So, we are stuck with having to contract out the anthropological study to the Bureau. It's going to cost us per diem and about two days' work to have some bureaucrat come up here and tell us what this idiot on staff could have told us over the phone.

We were told that the appraisal of the forty-acre piece, as well as the anthropological survey, would be done in November of 2000. Now the Bureau is telling us maybe the first of the year. I asked them if they could maybe pin that down a little better for me. I wanted to know if the first of the year meant the first week in January or the fourth week in May. Nobody could give me that answer. I hired a contractor to do the National Environmental Protection Act study. When that study is complete, and I file it with the tribe, I must provide a thirty-day public notice. Then the tribe writes what's called a "finding of no significant impact," a FONSI, which requires another thirty-day period for review.

Once those two things are done and if the appraisal, the environmental study, and the anthropological statement actually get accomplished, then and only then, can I go to visit the head bureaucrat in Everett. He has, of course, assured me that he can make the sign-off allowing me to install my sewer transmission line alongside George Lane down to my piece of property.

I've got cousins who live off that driveway. They have caused us nothing but heartache and grief. Last time I talked to one of them, we both threatened that the next time we saw each other, we were gonna kick each other's ass. I'm actually looking forward to that opportunity. We had to get restraining orders on several other cousins farther down the driveway who have threatened the workers. I call them renegades.

As a result of this latest holdup, Sue and I had to put in two extra holding tanks at the top of the drain field on our property down below. The sewage was supposed to go from the four tanks at the RV Park, into a manhole, under Highway 305, and down to the drain field. Now it gets trucked across the highway and seven-tenths of a mile down George Lane, where it's pumped into the two new tanks. There is a significantly higher risk of environmental catastrophe. The pipe that we put under 305 is just hanging there with the end capped.

When we do manage to wade through this latest pile of bureaucratic bull, and get a right-of-way to lay the pipe, we plan to flatten out the drain field and plant grass. We'll turn the drain field into a baseball and soccer field for the kids. Grandpa Benny would have had it no other way . . . never take anything without giving something back. Maybe we'll call it Shady Rest Ballpark. I'm sure that the spirit of my dad will be sitting up on the hill, taking a pull, and watching the game . . . far enough away, of course, so they don't ask him to umpire.

33 | Epilogue

THAT I HAD THE OPPORTUNITY AND GREAT HONOR TO WRITE EMERSON'S story was the start of a long string of coincidences. Emerson and I were born in the same hospital and graduated from high school in the same year. We both traveled up the Elwha River, up the Low Divide, across the skyline trail and down the North Fork of the Quinault River. We both hid in our sleeping bags from the bloodsucking swarm of mosquitoes at Lake Beauty. When Emerson's father quit the shipyard in protest over being required to pay dues to the Veterans Association, my father was Veterans Association president. Emerson and his wife Sue, unbeknownst to me, cared for my stepsister's son, David, for well over a decade. The guy that services my septic tank was Emerson's next-door neighbor growing up in Suquamish. When I suggested to Emerson that maybe a higher power had brought us together, he smiled and said, "I never question the way things are." So be it. Chief Sealth passed away on the 7th day of June 1866. Rumor has it that there were no Whites from "the town that bore his name" present at his funeral. He was buried in the tribal cemetery in Suquamish, Washington. Lyle Emerson George is of his blood.

and when the last Red man
shall have perished from the earth
and his memory among White men
shall have become a myth,
these shores will swarm with the invisible dead of my tribe
and when your children's children shall think themselves alone
in the field, the store, the shop, upon the highway,

or in the silence of the woods,
they will not be alone.
In all the earth there is no place dedicated to solitude.
At night, when the streets of your cities and villages
shall be silent and you think them deserted,
they will throng with the returning hosts
that once filled and still love this beautiful land.
The White man will never be alone.
Let him be just and deal kindly with my people,
for the dead are not powerless.

—JTW

Scouting offered me a stable environment. Eventually I attained the rank of Eagle Scout—the first in the history of Suquamish. (Emerson kneeling in front.)

In the Suquamish Elementary School, We were the only Indians in the class. (Emerson, first row, on the right) (Nelson, third row, fifth from left.)

At a meeting with Governor Lowry in the State Gaming Commission Office in Olympia.